FROM SHADOW TO SUBSTANCE

FROM SHADOW TO SUBSTANCE

the Rediscovery of the Inner Message of
the Epistle to the Hebrews, Centered
Around the Words "Let Us Go On"

ROY HESSION

ZONDERVAN
PUBLISHING HOUSE
OF THE ZONDERVAN CORPORATION | GRAND RAPIDS, MICHIGAN 49506

FROM SHADOW TO SUBSTANCE
Copyright © 1977 by The Zondervan Corporation
Grand Rapids, Michigan

Library of Congress Cataloging in Publication Data
Hession, Roy.
   From shadow to substance.
     1. Bible.   N.T.   Hebrews—Criticism,
interpretation, etc.   I.   Title.
BS2775.2.H47   227'.87'06   76-52750

Printed in the United States of America

Contents

Introduction . . . . — 9

1 *Let Us Go On*
From Shadow to Substance 17

2 *Let Us Go On*
From Living in the Wilderness
to Living in Canaan 27

3 *Let Us Go On*
From Knowing Jesus as Our Aaron
to Knowing Him as Our Melchizedek 53

4 *Let Us Go On*
From Living Under the Old Covenant
to Living Under the New 71

5 *Let Us Go On*
From Living in the Holy Place to Living
in the Holiest of All 91

6 Entering Into the Holiest 113

7 The Power of the Blood of Christ 125

8 The Alternative to Going On — Drawing Back 135

9 Enduring to the End 147

10 Is the Apostate Irrecoverable? 163

11 The Race Set Before Us 181

Appendix: The Versions Used 201

Acknowledgments

The following are the authors of verses used in this book.

28 — Author unknown
29 — Fanny J. Crosby
33a — Mary Shekleton
33b — Author unknown
36 — E. H. Hobkins
38 — Charles Wesley
45 — John Newton
56 — Author unknown
63 — C. L. Bancroft
64a — S. D. Phelps
64b — Charles Wesley
65 — P. J. Owens
66 — E. Mote
67 — Isaac Watts
77 — Author unknown
96 — Charles Wesley
106 — Authors unknown

108 — T. Binney
114 — A. M. Hull
120a — E. Caswall
120b — E. R. Latta
132 — Charles Wesley
148 — Author unknown
150 — Sir H. W. Baker
151 — A. M. Toplady
152 — E. C. Clephane
156 — Author unknown
159a — Fanny J Crosby
159b — John Newton
164a — W. Cowper
164b — Author unknown
176 — E. A. Hoffman
194 — E. M. Grimes
196 — W. Cowper

197 — Esther K. Rusthoi

For when for the time ye ought to be teachers, ye have need that one teach you again which be the first principles of the oracles of God; and are become such as have need of milk, and not of strong meat.

For everyone that useth milk is unskilful in the word of righteousness; for he is a babe.

But strong meat belongeth to them that are of full age, even those who by reason of use have their senses exercised to discern both good and evil.

Therefore leaving the first principles of the doctrines of Christ,
      let us go on unto full growth,
not laying again the foundation
      of repentance from dead works,
      and of faith toward God,
      of the doctrine of baptisms,
      and of laying on of hands,
      and of resurrection of the dead,
      and of eternal judgement.
And this will we do, if God permit.

— Hebrews 5:12–6:3

Introduction

IF THERE IS one part of a book that a reader ought to read first and more carefully than any other, it is the introduction, or preface, especially if it is written by the author. In it the author tells the reader what he is going to tell him and the reader can decide if he will be interested enough to read on. The story is told of a young man who, about to embark on preaching, went to a seasoned Methodist lay preacher for advice. "Well, first of all," said the old man, "I tells 'em wot I'm going to tell 'em; then I tells 'em; then I tells 'em wot I've told 'em."

That certainly is the purpose of this introduction, to let you know what to expect in these pages and to prepare your mind for them. If you are expecting something from a book and it is not there, you will not be in a state of mind to receive and benefit from what *is* there.

This book contains some very simple and practical studies in one of the most glorious writings in the New Testament — Paul's letter to the Hebrews. I will explain later why I accept the traditional view that Paul was its author. These studies are, in effect, rediscoveries which I feel I have been making of the inner message of this epistle. Indeed, in these last years, ever since the experience of revival began to come to my life, I think I can say I have embarked on a voyage of rediscovery of the gospel of the grace of God, which I thought I knew so well, but it was not at the level which I needed. These studies in no sense attempt anything like a complete exposition of this epistle. Whole portions of it are left untouched. What is attempted is to uncover the personal, practical message for every Christian that lies embedded in its pages — and that only. It will be found to be one of the most encouraging messages that weak, sometimes failing saints like ourselves can ever hear. The message this epistle contains is supremely an experiential message.

At first sight, the epistle does not seem to be all that practical or experiential; indeed, it seems to be mainly an epistle of doctrine. There is certainly plenty of doctrine in it. It contains more wonderful teaching of the Lord Jesus Christ and how He is the fulfillment of the Old Testament types than any other epistle in the New Testament. But if we look on this as only a doctrinal writing, we shall make a big mistake. It is not given us for our academic study. Paul did not regard it as an epistle of doctrine; he regarded it as an epistle of *exhortation.* In the last chapter (13:22) he says, "I beseech you, brethren, bear with the *word of exhortation,* for I have written a letter unto you in a few words." Whereas there is much about the Lord Jesus Christ and His work for us, it is given mainly as the ground on which Paul bases his very practical word of exhortation to them and us.

To exhort another is to urge, encourage, and warn him. We have all these three elements in the exhortations of this epistle, with its oft-repeated "let us . . . let us . . . let us. . . ." The central exhortation, what you may call the hub of the whole, is contained in 6:1: "Therefore leaving the first principles of the doctrine of Christ, let us go on unto full growth," or, as the Revised Standard Version translates it, "to maturity." The apostle urges them to "go on" because he knows that is the one thing they have not been doing and that instead of being spiritually full-grown they are still babes — a condition he describes in detail in the verses immediately preceding. Their condition was very much that of many a Christian today who has without doubt begun with Christ but not moved forward, and such a person needs the same exhortation to go on to maturity as was given to these Hebrew Christians of long ago.

Paul, however, not only urges them to "go on," but gives them every encouragement to do so, and that to the weakest of them. As I have said, the message of this epistle is just about the most encouraging thing on earth a needy Christian can hear. He may feel himself feeble and failing, but it tells him that every provision has been made by the God of grace for even such as he to go on into the fullness of His salvation. These provisions are for him as he is, rather than as he ought to be, and are made as accessible to faith as grace can make them.

On the other hand, these mighty encouragements to "go

on" are duly mixed with words of warning if he should fail to do so. The solemn word *lest* appears in a number of significant places and that is ever the word of warning. The warning is that if we do not *go on into grace*, we may *go back into sin* and that to lengths we never thought ourselves capable of, with disastrous consequences. We shall have to look carefully into this side of things later on in the book. It is, then, a very urgent writing for those tempted to draw back; but for those who see themselves poor and needy, it is a supremely encouraging one, for here we see Jesus as the sinner's Friend and High Priest.

Read, then, with a hungry heart, expecting to see Jesus as the answer to your need and willing to appropriate for yourself what you see and thus enter into further experience of His grace. Do not get too bogged down with the epistle itself. I would be disappointed myself if all you got was a new understanding of the epistle rather than a new sight of Jesus, and so would Paul, because that is what he wrote it for.

While on this point, may I say that, as I understand it, we do not come to Jesus through the Scriptures, but we come to the Scriptures through Jesus. Of course, the basic revelation of the Lord Jesus is in the Scriptures, but it needs the Holy Spirit to reveal Him to us personally. He will use the Scriptures to do so, but not only the Scriptures; sometimes it is somebody else's personal testimony that He uses to awaken our hearts, and nearly always our own deep experience of need, which is only to be met in Him. But having given us this personal experience of Jesus as the answer to our need, the Spirit then leads us back to the Scriptures and we see everywhere in its pages the Jesus we have come to know and the experience we have entered into, and the whole thing comes alive as it never did before.

It really is rather like the use we make of a guidebook. A guidebook gives us all sorts of information about a place and we gain some impression of that place, albeit a somewhat shadowy impression. When, however, we actually make the trip and visit the beautiful place, then what was shadowy to us before is now utterly real. We walk the streets, our eyes gaze on the beauties, and our nose smells the fragrance of the flowers. If we then turn back to the guidebook, we shall understand it as we never did before. When we return and want to describe to our friends what we have seen, we will doubtless make use of the guidebook. We will turn to its pages to express more adequately what we want to tell them, but we are not preaching the guidebook so much as what we have seen with our eyes; we are using the guidebook lest we have forgotten something or we get something wrong. Important as our experience of what we describe is, the guidebook is the final authority; but without the experience, it is not alive to us or to those we are speaking to. Does this illustration help you? If not, or if it raises more queries than it settles, then scrap it. But this I know, that in these pages I am not laboring to get you to understand an epistle as such, but rather sharing with you a life-transforming vision of Jesus revealed by the Spirit in my many hours of need and which I find gloriously set forth in this epistle, as indeed I find it all over the Bible.

As you will have noticed, I have been blithely speaking of Paul as the writer of this epistle, in spite of the fact that it is fashionable today to doubt his authorship. However, the authorship of Paul is the traditional view, as taken by the King James Version (also called the Authorized Version), and those early translators put his name in the title at the head. There it still stands in every edition of that great version: "The Epistle of Paul the Apostle to the Hebrews." Modern scholars, however, have doubted whether he was the writer and have all sorts of ideas as to who it was. Presumably, what has given the occasion for their doubts and speculations is the fact that his name does not actually appear in the text, as it does in all his other epistles. The result has been that preachers as a rule have been inhibited about ever saying, when speaking of this epistle, "Paul said this," or "Paul said that," and have preferred to say, "The writer to the Hebrews. . . ." Well, without apology, I am going to take the traditional view and say Paul throughout. The authorship of Paul is a very, very ancient tradition, and it was for this reason that the translators of the King James Version put his name at the head of the epistle. All I personally can say is that the more I read it, the more I hear the voice of Paul. I have lived with Paul and his writings for fifty years (ever since I came to know the Lord Jesus) and I can tell his accent anywhere. This is not Peter's accent, nor is it John's. Peter was a much simpler man than Paul.

Most interesting light is thrown on the circumstances and purpose of this writing by a little note that the King James Version adds at the end: "Written to the Hebrews from Italy by Timothy"; that is, it was presumably taken down by him at Paul's dictation and carried by him back to Judea. That, of course, is not part of the inspired text, but another ancient tradition. And it does seem so right. Paul suffered much from the Hebrews. They hated his gospel of free grace; it let the Gentiles in on the ground floor and seemed to make nothing of their own privileges. Because of their opposition, Paul was sent as a prisoner to Rome. But he loved those Hebrews, his kinsmen. He was willing to "wish himself accursed from Christ . . . that they might be saved." How natural, then, that he should write this epistle back to those beloved Hebrews to try to show them once again that Jesus really was the Messiah and the fulfillment of all the Old Testament prophecies.

There was a reason why he should not put his name to this letter. There were many Hebrews who believed in Jesus but who were nonetheless still zealous for the law of Moses (we will look later on at the passage that tells us this — Acts 21:20). They were in a complete muddle, and they were not at all sure how they viewed Paul. And so he writes this letter back to them from Rome. But he does not put his name to the letter because he knows they are prejudiced against him and they may not so readily receive his message. But any of them who knew him at all personally would say, "I know this is Paul, all right."

Enough of that!

The supreme thing is that here we have the Holy Spirit making a glorious revelation of the Lord Jesus as the "hope of every contrite heart," the "joy of all the meek."

By way of preparation for the following chapters, we will need a clear understanding of the meaning — a definition, if you like to call it that — of the word *grace*, which so often appears in these pages. Indeed, we have already used the word on a previous page: "If we do not *go on into grace*, we may *go back into sin.*" What does it mean? It is not merely a sense of spiritual well-being such as we receive at, say, a communion service. Nor is it, first, help given by God to undergo trials, though that is one sense of the word. It is, first of all, a glorious element in the divine character, just as love is: only in the case of grace, the object of the divine solicitude is always the unattractive, the incapable, and, above all, the undeserving. Unless you see yourself as that, you just do not qualify for the grace of God. The whole point of the grace God shows to man is that it is undeserved. Grace would not be grace if it were otherwise. "And if it be of grace, it is no more of works; otherwise grace is no more grace" (Rom. 11:6). In God's vocabulary, the opposite of sin is not goodness on man's part, but grace on His part. The call to do good where we have done evil only leads to self-effort, that is, to nowhere. But the message of grace brings us to the foot of the cross, there to have poured upon us the riches He has for us.

Keep this meaning of the word in mind as we explore together "the manifold grace of God" and its many implications for us.

Roy Hession

Note: For an explanation of the versions of the Scriptures used, see appendix, "The Versions Used."

Let Us Go On

From Shadow to Substance

. . . who serve unto the example and shadow of heavenly things. . . .

. . . the patterns of things in the heavens . . . the heavenly things themselves. . . .

For the law having a shadow of good things to come, and not the very image of the things. . . .

. . . which are a shadow of things to come; but the body is of Christ.

— Hebrews 8:5; 9:23; 10:1; Colossians 2:17

1

Let Us Go On
From Shadow to Substance

THERE IS A big difference between the shadow of an object and the object itself. Shadows can be beautiful, as when, for instance, a summer day draws toward the late afternoon and trees cast long shadows, greatly enhancing the scene. A visitor to the tropics is advised not to take his photographs at midday when the sun is immediately overhead, but in the afternoon when there are at least some shadows. But the shadows are at best only shadows, with no substance to them. The stately palm tree is of far greater importance and beauty than the shadow it casts, and no one would prefer the latter to the former. And yet that is just what the Hebrew Christians, to whom this epistle was written, were doing in their spiritual lives; they were contenting themselves with the shadow rather than the substance. And we shall see, as we proceed with our study, that the professed Christian today can be doing much the same.

The Hebrew Christians to whom Paul wrote were in a very strange condition. Presumably, they were the same believers that Paul found on his last visit to Jerusalem, when Peter warned Paul to be careful in his approach to them. Said he, "Thou seest, brother, how many thousands of Jews there are which believe; and they are all zealous of the law: and they are informed of thee, that thou teachest all the Jews which are among the Gentiles to forsake Moses, saying they ought not to circumcise their children, neither to walk after the customs" (Acts 21:20,21). What a confused position they were in! On the one hand, they had believed on the Lord Jesus as their Messiah, and yet, on the other hand, they were still zealous for the law of Moses, still performing the Old Testament rituals, and still offering the Old Testament sacrifices. So zealous were they for the law that they were incensed with Paul, if he ever implied that the grace of God had set aside that law. They had apparently not seen that those rituals were but "the shadows of good things to come" (or rather of *Him* who was to come) and that, now that He and those good things had indeed come, there was no need of shadows.

In the Acts of the Apostles there were other groups who seem to be in this in-between position. In 15:5 we read, "But there rose up certain of the sect of the *Pharisees* that believed." Although they had truly believed on Jesus as their Messiah — a big step indeed in view of what their rulers had done to Him — they were still very much Pharisees, as their insistence on the rite of circumcision for the Gentile believers showed and were therefore still occupied with the shadows.

Then in Acts 6:7 we find that "a great company of the priests were obedient to the faith." Did these newly converted priests continue nonetheless as priests and still offer "the same sacrifices that can never take away sins," or did they immediately go on from the shadows to the Substance? To have done the latter would have been very costly and would have provoked a furor indeed. I have the feeling that not all of them did so and therefore they must be included among those for whom this epistle is intended.

So Paul writes to all of them to expound just this — that these things, though divinely ordained in the first place, were only shadows of the real thing and not the real thing itself. Indeed, they were never intended to be anything else. In one place in this epistle he says that the Old Testament priests "serve unto the example and shadow of heavenly things" (8:5); in another place he speaks of "the law having a shadow of good things to come, and not the very image of them" (10:1). It was those good things to come which cast a shadow before them, but when the good things have come, who would want to be occupied with their shadow? It is somewhat like the shadow which the principle character in a play might cast before him just prior to his first entry. He pauses in the wings with a bright light shining behind him, causing his shadow to be cast right across the stage. All this adds to the dramatic effect of his entry. For the moment, the shadow is all the audience sees. They can see the shape of the actor and know that he is carrying a sword. But when he actually steps onto the stage, they see the substance of which all they had seen before was but shadow — and their interest in the shadow disappears.

For long centuries Jesus Christ had stood in the wings of history. He was God's promised One and with Him were good things to come — the good things of man's redemption. But as He stood there, He cast His shadow before Him right through the pages of the Old Testament. The law of Moses with its priesthood, sacrifices, and rituals was just that shadow. Those things were all types and foreshadowings of Him who was to come. They were preparing the people for their Messiah. How else would the people have understood what John the Baptist meant when he said of Him, "Behold the Lamb of God that taketh away the sin of the world"? The people had been offering lambs all down the years as an atonement for their sin. They had therefore become familiar with the thought that "without the shedding of blood there is no remission." All that, however, was but a shadow of what was to come. But now John saw that the substance had come, the Lord Jesus Himself, who on the cross of Calvary was going to bear away the sin of the world. This is exactly what Paul meant when he wrote to the Colossians on the same subject: ". . . which are a shadow of things to come, but the body [which casts the shadow] is of Christ" (Col. 2:17). I am sure that John the Baptist never wanted to offer another lamb in the temple once he had seen Jesus. He had found reality. He had gone on from shadow to Substance.

But not so these Hebrew Christians. Although they had believed on the Lord Jesus and "endured a great fight of afflictions" on His behalf at the hands of their countrymen and had shown various other evidences that they had really begun with Him (see 6:4,5; 6:9; 10:32-34), they had not gone on from the shadows to the substance; they were still largely occupied with the law of Moses and its ritual.

For this reason their experience of grace was a shadowy one; indeed, it was much more an experience of the law than that of the grace of God. They were spiritual babes rather than full-grown Christians, and Paul had to say to them, "When for the time ye ought to be teachers, ye have need that one teach you again which be the first principles of the oracles of God; and are become such as have need of milk, and not of strong meat." Furthermore, in that position they were in danger, if they did not go on to the substance, of yielding up under the pressure of persecution the little they had. Again and again in this epistle the contrasted possibility is put before them of either going on from the shadow to the substance or of "departing from the living God" altogether and "drawing back to perdition" (3:12; 10:39).

THE SHADOW CHRISTIAN LIFE

I think we can look upon the shadow and substance as picturing two sorts of Christian lives. There is a Christian life, if we can call it such, which is just a shadow of the real thing; things spiritual are not real to the one trying to live it; the whole thing is an effort which leads only to emptiness. In British politics, we talk of the "Shadow Cabinet." The party in opposition, not in power, duplicates the government's Cabinet of Ministers. They are doubtless splendid men with splendid plans, but not being in power, they are unable to implement their plans. Well, the shadow Christian life is the same — good intentions and promises, but no power, no reality.

Such a Christian life can nonetheless be a very active one in God's service. We can be much involved in the life of the church, teaching in Sunday school, singing in the choir, taking part in the visitation program, sitting on committees, making the tea, pouring the coffee — or even preaching the sermons; but we can do all these things with a heart that is not experiencing the reality of what is promised in the Bible. These are but shadows of the real thing, and not the real thing itself. As one looks on it all, he is sometimes constrained to say, but where is Jesus in all this? He Himself is the true substance, but all we seem to see so often is His shadow.

The shadow is, of course, linked with the object; it has very much the same shape and could not exist apart from that of which it is the shadow. But it is nonetheless only a shadow, there is nothing of substance to it. So of the shadow Christian life and its activities. They are linked with Jesus Christ; we can discern something of His shape from them, and they could hardly exist apart from Him, whose shadow they are. But they are only shadows of the real. And who would be content with the shadows when he can possess and be possessed by the Substance? But when we are in fact content only with the shadows, our condition is very much the same as that of the Hebrew Christians in this epistle, that of babes instead of deeply rooted men and women of God, and we are in the same danger as they were of going back on our confession of faith when real pressure comes.

How actually does the Epistle to the Hebrews describe the way by which we go on from shadow to substance? This is the subject of later chapters of this present writing, but we cannot close this chapter without at least a glimpse of the way. The answer is faith, and faith is here described as "the substance of things hoped for" (11:1). But faith in what, or in whom? Obviously in Jesus — but, note it, in Jesus as the Savior and High Priest of sinners. This means that I must admit that I am a sinner if I am to qualify for such a Savior and inasmuch as I am dealing with a holy God, vague generalizations of my sinfulness will not do. He will pin me down to this and that matter wherein I have shown myself a sinner. As I humble myself to repent and be honest about it, I become a candidate for that grace of God which is brought to me in Jesus, in a way I never was before. This, then, is where reality comes in. In the shadow Christian life we are not real with God. Having a legal view of Him, we feel we cannot afford to be real about ourselves, and as a result He is not real to us. At Sinai, where God's law was annunciated and where our blessing is dependent on obedience to it, we cannot afford to be wrong. We are in for a thrashing if we are! But at Calvary, "mercy there was great and grace was free; pardon there was multiplied to me; there my burdened soul found liberty." There the sinner can afford to be real and, to his joy and relief, Jesus in turn becomes real to him.

One word of warning here. You must be sure you have not got the wrong mental picture of what the substance, the reality, is going to be. Simeon, an old Levite in the temple, was "waiting for the consolation of Israel"; that means he was expecting in his day the appearing of the Messiah and of all that that would mean for Israel. Indeed, the record says that it was revealed to him by the Holy Spirit that he should not see death before he had seen the Lord's Christ. When he did see Him, all he saw was a little baby brought by a poor peasant woman. How easy it would have been for him to have had the wrong mental picture of what the Messiah was going to be and therefore to see nothing of any special significance in this event, and turn away. Instead, he took Him up in his arms and blessed God, saying, "Mine eyes have seen thy salvation." Simeon was holding that day the Substance, the eternal Reality in his arms. If you like, he was holding revival in his arms, the victorious life in his arms, the answer to every man's need in his arms. We sometimes have the wrong mental picture of what revival is, or what the victorious Christian life is likely to be in experience, or how our needs are going to be met. Very often we have in mind something that will be spectacular, sudden, powerful. If we have the wrong mental picture, we will never find what we are looking for. We need to see that Jesus is revival and everything else we need, even though He appears small and His fresh working to be at first in but one heart, our own. After all, revival has to begin somewhere and beginnings are always small. But if you do not see Him as such, you will not even have that beginning. Indeed, in your anxiety for the answer, you may take up something else in your arms — a new emphasis, a new doctrine, a new experience — and though for a time you will feel yourself satisfied, you will ultimately find that even that is but shadow and not the substance.

OUTSIDE THE CAMP

For the Hebrew Christians to go on from shadow to substance would be very costly, for it would be a "going forth unto him without the camp" of Judaism, and that would not be appreciated, to put it mildly, by the rest of the people who made so much of Judaism. These Christians had already brought upon themselves severe persecution as a result of acknowledging Him whom the nation had crucified, but finally to forsake Judaism as a religious system would involve them in much worse. Let us look at the verses to which we are alluding: "Wherefore Jesus also, that he might sanctify the people with his own blood, suffered without the gate. Let us go therefore unto him without the camp, bearing his reproach" (13:12, 13). Jesus had suffered at the hands of Judaism without the gate; if they too went outside the camp, they could not but bear the same reproach as that which fell on Him.

It can be costly for us too to go on from the shadow to the substance, because it will mean going outside the camp of much which is highly esteemed among religious people, and we will certainly not be popular and may well find ourselves bearing the reproach of Christ. This does not mean that we will necessarily leave our church or denomination, but it may well mean that we will not be the ardent denominationalists we once were, nor perhaps put the same heavy emphasis on the sacraments we used to, or be as much enamored of the latest bit of evangelical "methodology" as some would have us be, for we see these things to be but shadows of the real thing and not the Real Thing Himself. On the other hand, we may be guided by God not to give up what we now see to be mere shadows, but actually to identify ourselves with them, if only to help others there to find the substance, that is, to find Jesus Christ. This is just what Paul did: "Though I was free from all men, I brought myself under bondage to all, that I might gain the more. And to the Jews I became as a Jew, that I might gain the Jews; to them that are under the law, as under the law, not being myself under the law, that I might gain them that are under the law" (1 Cor. 9:19,20). But even so, the shadows can never mean very much to us once we have found the substance. Let us go on, then, from shadow to substance, cost what it may by way of reproach.

This, then, is a first general overall look at our theme, "Let us go on." As we move further into this epistle, we will see there are four clearly defined things *to* which we are to go on and therefore four equally clearly defined things *from* which we are to go.

Let Us Go On

From Living in the Wilderness
to Living in Canaan

. . . but Christ as a son over his own house; whose house are we, if we hold fast the confidence and the rejoicing of the hope firm unto the end.

Wherefore (as the Holy Spirit saith, Today if ye will hear his voice, harden not your hearts, as in the provocation, in the day of temptation in the wilderness: when your fathers tempted me, proved me, and saw my works forty years. Wherefore I was grieved with that generation, and said, They do alway err in their heart; and they have not known my ways; as I sware in my wrath, They shall not enter into my rest.) Take heed, brethren, lest there be in any of you an evil heart of unbelief, in departing from the living God. But exhort one another daily, while it is called Today; lest any of you be hardened through the deceitfulness of sin.

For we are made partakers of Christ, if we hold the beginning of our confidence steadfast unto the end; while it is said, Today if ye will hear his voice, harden not your hearts, as in the provocation. For who when they heard did provoke? Nay, did not all they that came out of Egypt by Moses? And with whom was he grieved forty years? Was it not with them that sinned, whose carcases fell in the wilderness? And to whom sware he that they should not enter into rest, but to them that believed not? So we see that they could not enter in because of unbelief.

Let us therefore fear, lest, a promise being left us of entering into rest, any of you should seem to come short of it. For unto us was good tidings preached, as well as unto them: but the word preached did not profit them, not being mixed with faith in them that heard it. For we which have believed do enter into rest. . . .

Seeing therefore it remaineth that some must enter therein, and they to whom it was first preached entered not in because of unbelief, he again defineth a certain day, saying in David, Today, after so long a time, as it is written. Today if ye will hear his voice, harden not your hearts. For if Joshua had given them rest, then would he not afterward have spoken of another day.

There remaineth therefore a sabbath rest to the people of God. For he that is entered into his rest, he also hath ceased from his own works, as God did from his.

Let us labour therefore to enter into that rest, lest any man fall after the same example of unbelief.

— Hebrews 3:6–4:11

2

Let Us Go On

From Living in the Wilderness to Living in Canaan

AS WE HAVE seen, Paul is addressing a people who in their Christian lives had begun but had not gone on. In chapters 3 and 4 of this epistle he illustrates the position they were in by likening it to the position of their fathers when they had been brought out of the bondage of Egypt, but had failed to enter into the land of Canaan which God had promised them. They were somewhere in between — in the desert of Sinai and that for no less than forty years. Theirs was a pathetic case of stopping short of the good thing God had purposed. Paul sees that as exactly the position of his readers and he writes to urge them to go on from living in the spiritual (or unspiritual) counterpart of the wilderness to living in the spiritual counterpart of Canaan and to give them every encouragement to do so.

That long period in the wilderness was never God's first purpose for them. When He redeemed them out of the slavery of Egypt, it was not merely to save them from the whip of Pharaoh but to bring them into a much better land, a land that flowed with milk and honey, a land of mountains and rivers and of easy fruitfulness, wherein they could eat bread without scarceness. As Moses said in Deuteronomy 6:23, "He brought us out from thence that he might bring us in."

However, to get into that land the whole people had to go through the wilderness of Sinai, and it was a very difficult desert. When they first tasted freedom, they were full of confidence in their great Jehovah who had so wonderfully brought them out. On the eastern bank of the Red Sea they sang their song of praise to Him and joyfully anticipated their entering into the land that He had promised them. But that newfound faith was much tested in the wilderness, and it did not stand up. Whenever conditions in the desert were difficult, they doubted in their hearts, murmured against what God had allowed and the leader He had given them, and would gladly have turned back to Egypt, had that been possible. Little wonder that God said, "Wherefore I was grieved with that generation"! The climax of their unbelief and rebelliousness came at Kadesh-Barnea, when they were on the very borders of the promised land. Because of the report of fortified cities and men of great stature in the land, they doubted God once again and positively refused to go in and do battle. They even got as far as looking around for a leader who would take them back to Egypt. It was then that God uttered a terrible oath, that none of that generation would go into that land. For forty years they were to wander up and down the desert, until all that generation had died, and after that He would bring their children into the land. And so it was that the wilderness was strewed with their bones. Only two men of the original great company that had come out of Egypt made Canaan.

> Joshua, the son of Nun,
> And Caleb, the son of Jephunneh,
>   Were the only two
>   Who ever got through,
> To the land of milk and honey.

Now these things were meant to be types and figures of ourselves. All of us were born into a society ruled over by the counterpart of Pharaoh, i.e., Satan, whom Paul elsewhere describes as "the god of this world." But God purposed to have a people for Himself saved out of the world, and through the redemption of His Son He has that people.

The manner of Israel's redemption is a picture of ours. They were redeemed both by blood and by power. The blood of the lamb sprinkled on the doorposts of their houses saved them from sharing the divine judgment on Egypt and the miracle of the parting of the Red Sea and its convenient return to drown the Egyptians saved them from the power of Pharaoh. For this redemption, Israel sang praises to God as they never had before. But the Lord Jesus has accomplished an even greater emancipation for us. Through His blood sprinkled on our guilty hearts by our repentance and faith He has saved us from sharing in the divine judgment of the world; and by the right hand of His power He has lifted us up and delivered us from our old life in that world. As a result there is today a redeemed, blood-bought people who sing:

> Redeemed, how I love to proclaim it,
> Redeemed by the blood of the Lamb
> Redeemed by His infinite mercy
> His child, and for ever, I am.

Now what is God's purpose in bringing us out of Egypt? It is not something negative; it is something gloriously positive — to bring us into all the fullness of the Lord Jesus, where all the longings of our hearts are more than satisfied by fellowship with Himself, where we find Him truly the Bread of Life and the Water of Life, where we see Him putting to flight our enemies and giving us victory over sin and Satan. Very often our hymns picture Canaan as heaven, but in the passage set out at the beginning of this chapter Canaan is something we are to enter now. In the passage and its context, the word *today* comes as many as five times. Therefore, Canaan, it seems, pictures that life of satisfaction and liberty which Jesus has for us "today."

So often, however, we find that we stop between the two. There are times when I know quite surely I am out of Egypt, but I am not in Canaan. I may have tasted that joy long ago, but at the moment I cannot say I have it as I did then. I am somewhere between; I am in the wilderness, and the wilderness can be a very unpleasant place. Sometimes the Israelites said, "We were happier in Egypt than in this place," and sometimes Christians can get so low that they say, "We were happier before we were converted than in this terrible wilderness we are in as Christians." On the other hand, we can get so used to the wilderness that we are content to go on living there. We have perhaps never known much else, and we are tempted to say, "Perhaps that is all Jesus meant me to have." But it cannot possibly be God's purpose that we should be in the wilderness with no song and satisfaction in our hearts and brought again and again under the guilt of sin. He brought us out that He might bring us in. Nothing else will satisfy His heart — nor ours. Whatever may be our present experience, let us tell ourselves, there is somewhere, somehow, a promised land which grace has reserved for us in Christ.

What Is Canaan?

Now what is this life which is pictured for us by Canaan? If we can establish from this passage what it really means, we will by contrast see what the wilderness is in which we sometimes find ourselves wandering and we will be better able to appreciate the way by which we may enter and enjoy the promised land.

In warning the Hebrew Christians of the danger of not going on, Paul quotes in chapter 3 from Psalm 95, where God swears that the children of Israel shall not enter into His rest, that is, the promised Canaan. Then he goes on to say (and this is most important), "For we are made partakers of Christ if we hold the beginning of our confidence steadfast unto the end" (3:14). Apparently then, the promised land for the Christian is being "made a partaker of Christ." Note, not merely an imitator of Christ, nor even a servant of Christ, but a partaker of Christ. And what I partake of, as in the case of something I eat, becomes mine in a way nothing else does. So this is a union with Christ, where He becomes mine, where His life is mine, where His power is mine, where His position of ascendancy over His enemies is mine, where His love for others is mine; in short, where He lives again His life in me as I am joined to

Him. By any showing, that is victory. It is not my life being improved, but rather His life being imparted. Someone has said, "There is only one victorious life in the world and that is the life of the victorious Christ, which He wants to live again in us." The Lord Jesus Himself, then, is our Canaan.

Now this verse tells us the condition on which we are made partakers of Christ. It says that this becomes so only "*if* we hold fast the beginning of our confidence steadfast unto the end.*" Apparently, it is not a once-for-all experience. I am made a partaker of Christ only *if* — and this condition could be fulfilled one day and not the next. The important thing is how it is with me right now, and after this now, the next now. Apparently, the experience of Canaan is a continuous and contemporary one; that little word *if* makes that clear.

But if what? — "if we hold fast the beginning of our confidence steadfast unto the end." Note, not if we hold the beginning of our determination steadfast unto the end; nor, if we hold the beginning of our consecration steadfast unto the end; but if we hold the "beginning of our confidence steadfast unto the end." Now when we come across this word *confidence* or *faith* in the New Testament, we must always ask ourselves, faith or confidence in what? Faith is a colorless word apart from its object. Considered by themselves, what do such statements as these mean: "Oh woman, great is thy faith," or, "I have prayed for thee that thy faith fail not," or, the phrase in our verse here, "the beginning of your confidence . . . "? Confidence in what? It is not enough to say it is confidence in God or in Jesus. Everything depends on what our conception of the Deity is before you can say that. It is no use telling a man to trust in the Lord, if deep down his conception of the Deity is of one who cannot but have the big stick for a man as failing as he is. In that case, you are only asking a man to believe more firmly in his own condemnation than ever!

I believe that in passage after passage where "faith" or "confidence" is used, *grace* is implied as its object. It is faith in the grace of God for sinners that makes the self-acknowledged sinner bold to draw near. It is confidence in the immutability of that grace which brings the saint who has failed yet again back into fellowship with God. We are certainly called to put faith in the power of God, but more often in His grace, just because of the many states of need and culpability we find ourselves in. The leper said to Jesus, "If Thou wilt, Thou canst make me clean." He believed in Christ's power — that He *could;* but he had doubts about His grace — whether He *would.* He doubted whether such a dirty leper as he qualified for so great a blessing as he was asking. Faith in grace was a new thing to him; he knew as yet so little about the Lord.

This was where the Gentile woman, the Syrophoenecian, triumphed. She had such an insight into the grace of His heart that she did not resent His description of her as a dog ("It is not meet to take the children's bread," Jesus had said, "and give it to dogs"); she was prepared to take her place as a Gentile dog because she saw in it a qualification for that grace that specializes in the unprivileged and the poor and needy, and dared to say, "The dogs eat the crumbs that fall from their masters' tables." Jesus could not resist her when she spoke like that and said, "Oh woman, great is your faith in my grace! Have it as you will: your daughter is whole." The simple truth is that *grace can never resist faith in itself.*

So here in the verse we are considering, we are told to hold fast the beginning of our confidence in grace firm to the end. Faith in grace surely was the beginning of our confidence when we first came out of Egypt. We saw ourselves as sinners without hope in ourselves. Every effort to redeem ourselves by self-improvement only ended in failure and added to our sense of condemnation. Then Jesus came, the embodiment of the grace of God, and we saw that He had something for sinners just in our condition; indeed, what He had was only for such. A confidence in that grace grew up in our hearts, we admitted the truth about ourselves, and came to Him — and He brought us out of Egypt. It was as simple and surprising and as quick as that. If it be of grace, then it is no more of works, and there need be no time-lag.

That was the beginning of our confidence, was it not? and that is the confidence which we have to hold steadfast to the end. It will be this confidence in God's grace for sinners that will bring us out of the wilderness into Canaan. We are to see that grace has made Jesus available to us as we are; there are no spiritual heights to climb or depths to plumb first; all we need is the brokenness that admits the place in the wilderness where we are, and thus we come to Him. We certainly have to take the witness box against ourselves in His presence in all honesty, but as we do so, His blood cleanses what we confess and grace brings us into Canaan and makes us partakers of Christ.

And this is the way we continuously partake of Christ. The life and fullness of the Lord Jesus are made available to us always on the ground of grace. No efforts or improvements on our part are necessary for us to qualify. All we need is the confession to Him of emptiness and need. Under grace confessed emptiness is ever the qualification to be filled. Only when you know how to hold the beginning of your confidence in grace firm to the end, will you dare to use Mary Shekleton's words all along the way:

> I am an empty vessel — not one thought,
> Or look of love, I ever to Thee brought;
> But I may come, and come again to Thee,
> With this, the empty sinner's only plea,
> Thou lovest me.

There may be failures and falling short in Canaan, but embracing this confidence, we know that all such things have been anticipated and provided for in the Lord Jesus and that

> Grace there is my every debt to pay,
> Blood to wash my every sin away.

One who has this confidence will not despair and give up hope when he falls or feels low; he knows how to repent and to come to Jesus again. He has a holy confidence in the mighty efficacy of the grace of God to bring a sinner like him into fullness again.

The opposite to "holding fast the beginning of our confidence steadfast unto the end" is found in 10:35 where we read, "Cast not away your confidence which hath great recompense of reward." The contrast is between holding this confidence in grace steadfast to the end or casting it away, and of course the hour of failure is the time when we are most tempted to do this and despair. This is precisely what Satan wants us to do; indeed, this is the very reason why he engineered the failure — not merely that we might do something unethical, but that he might now have the opportunity to accuse us and tell us there is no hope. This was the very thing that Jesus was concerned that Peter should not do in the hour of his failure. Jesus said to him, "Satan hath desired to have thee that he might sift thee as wheat; but I have prayed for thee, that thy faith fail not; and when thou art converted [or hast turned again] strengthen thy brethren." Apparently Peter was going to endure a great test of faith. Obviously, it was the hour of his failure in denying the Lord that is referred to here, and it was going to be faith in the immutability of the grace of God that was going to be tested. In the hour of failure could he still believe that grace had a hope for him or would he cast away his confidence? The man who knows how to hold fast this hope in grace knows what to do when failure, large or small, comes. Unlike Judas, he does not despair and wish to end his Christian life, but like Peter, he weeps, repents, and returns to the Lord and then goes on, rejoicing and free, partaking of the life and fullness of Jesus, who lives in him.

Obviously, if Canaan means being made a partaker of Christ, and if it is only by continuing to hold fast our confidence in grace that we continually partake of His life and fullness, then we shall have to be those who continually qualify for that grace by being willing continually to see sin as sin, as the Lord may show it to us. To illustrate, I once found in the flyleaf of my first wife's Bible a little sheet with a list of words one under another, such as bossiness, nagging, worry, tenseness, lack of caring for others, reserve, and other such. I asked her what this list meant. She said, "They are the things that God has from time to time shown me in my heart to be sin and I keep the list there to check as to whether I am still seeing them as sin." Note, not to check whether or not they were coming back — because she was human, such reactions might on occasions come back — but whether, if and when they did, she was continuing to see them as sin. In other words, was she holding the attitude with which she began steadfast to the end? There may be some people, of course, who feel they have got beyond the need to repent of things they have once seen as sin; they do not feel they are bothered by them now and it is a long time since they had to repent. But could it be that these things are there all right, but they are not seeing them as sin, as they once did, and therefore are not holding fast to the end that attitude of repentance and faith in grace with which they began? Even if there is no specific sin for me to see, I am still in myself "an empty vessel," empty of holiness, love, and power, and I need to be coming to Jesus to confess that fact if I am to know His fullness continuously.

I am well aware that this conception of living in the fullness of Jesus will come as a surprise to many and that some will hate it. Quite frankly, from some points of view, I hate it too. I do not find it easy to be broken again in repentance, and I would much rather not have to go on repenting and coming again to the throne of grace as a sinner. But my experience tells me it is the only way to holiness and to be continuously a partaker of the Lord Jesus.

This is why there is such a heavy emphasis in this passage on "today." It matters not that I came out of Egypt and entered into Canaan in the past; it is what is happening today that matters. "Today," if I hear His voice, I am not to harden my heart and be like the children of Israel in the wilderness (3:7). "Today" I need my brother to exhort and challenge me lest I be hardened through the deceitfulness of sin (3:13). "Today, after so long a time" (4:7), He calls me again to return.

Canaan, then, is simply living with Jesus in the now. If that be so, it may be misleading even to speak of "entering into Canaan." All we have to do from the day of our initial conversion to God is to hold the beginning of that confidence steadfast to the end and we are in Canaan. In actual fact, we may not always do so, and only because of that do we find ourselves in the wilderness, and need to enter again into our Canaan.

All this is called in our passage "His rest." In chapters 3 and 4 this word occurs no fewer than eleven times, usually in the phrase, "entering into His rest." Entering into Canaan was certainly rest for the children of Israel — a rest from constant packing and unpacking, and living out of suitcases! But their ultimate entering into Canaan under Joshua did not exhaust the promise of rest which God had in mind when He used the phrase in Psalm 95 "enter into my rest." Paul says, "For if Joshua had given them rest, then would he not afterwards have spoken of another day" as he does in Psalm 95. He concludes, therefore, that "there remaineth a rest to the people of God" (4:9), and it is still waiting for us today. He goes further and describes the character of this rest, "for he that has entered into God's rest has ceased from his own works, as God did from His" (4:10). God rested from His work of creation on the Sabbath day; and Jesus, when He had completed our redemption, rested from that work too, knowing that it was enough to bring an infinite number of sons to glory. "Having offered one sacrifice for sins for ever, He sat down" (10:12) and we are invited to enter into His rest and cease from our own works as God and Jesus did from Theirs. This means resting from the weary way of trying to find in ourselves a holiness which can only be found in Christ. But, as we shall see in later pages, the work that was necessary to bring us into perfect peace and fellowship with God has already been done, and Jesus is resting about it, even if we are not, and He longs that we enter into His rest too.

> My Saviour, Thou hast promised rest,
>   Oh, give it then to me,
> The rest of ceasing from myself,
>   To find my all in Thee.

WHAT IS THE WILDERNESS?

We are now by contrast able to see what living in the wilderness is. It is the reverse of what we have seen living in Canaan to be. Instead of finding our holiness in Christ, we are seeking to find it in ourselves. The latter is what we are always doing in the wilderness, trying to find something in ourselves on which to build our hopes of peace, some evidences of faith, or feeling, or goodness, and knowing only condemnation of heart when we fail to find it there. This in turn leads to despair, and if the despairing one does not see and believe that there is yet grace for the sinner, he may get to the place where he will want to finish with the Christian life altogether. To be in the wilderness, then, is to be in a position of grave peril. It is for this reason that Paul in these two chapters addresses to the Hebrews the most solemn warnings: "Take heed, brethren, lest there be in any of you an evil heart of unbelief, in departing from the living God" (3:12); and again: "Let us fear, therefore, lest, a promise being left us of entering into his rest, any of you should seem to come short of it" (4:1); and yet again: "Let us labour therefore to enter into that rest, lest any man fail after the same example of unbelief" (4:11).

The fact is that God does not give us any hope of finding holiness in ourselves. Our human nature since the Fall has become dominated by what Paul calls in his other epistles "the flesh," that is, the self-centered principle that came into man's being when he committed the first sin. All the splendid faculties of the human personality, what the Bible calls the soul, have now become controlled by the self-principle and prostituted to its service. We look in vain for that nature to produce a spiritual love for God and our fellows, or any power to live the Christian life. The attempt to find those things there will be a most discouraging experience, no matter how earnest we may be. Paul tried it and he ended up by confessing, "To will is present with me, but how to perform that which is good I find not" (Rom. 7:18). His intentions were good but his performance nil. What looked like the beginnings of holiness always broke down under test. It was one of the Puritan writers, I think, who said, "It is easier to get oil out of a stone than holiness out of the flesh."

Not only is the flesh incapable of producing holiness, but what it does produce with the greatest of ease is the very opposite — self-centered actions and reactions. This is what is native to human nature. And self-centeredness is simply another name for sin. It is not without significance that the central letter of the little word *sin* is *I*. You can see the dark catalog of the works of the flesh, seventeen of them, in Galatians 5, beginning with adultery, going on through more polite things, such as contention and strife, to not-so-polite drunkenness and revelings. But it is all the flesh, whether polite or impolite, and equally abhorrent to God. The flesh is the same in the believer as in the unbeliever, and the terrible thing is that it can intrude even into the service of God. This lies at the bottom of the deadness and unhappiness of some of our churches — the flesh in the service of God. A pastor's son, whose father had suffered much in the strife of tongues in his church, said, "Dad, I think the text 'Where two or three are gathered together in my name, there am I in the midst' ought to be rewritten. It should read, 'Where two or three are gathered together in my name, there is bound to be trouble.' " The shame of it!

And all the time, the Holy Spirit is abiding in the one who is born again, and because of His availability, there is no need for the believer to continue the weary business of trying to make the flesh a better Christian, or to allow it to express itself in its characteristic way. The Holy Spirit is within, not to improve the flesh, but rather to bring it to the judgment of the Cross and to supplant it with the life, love, and power of Jesus Himself — and that is holiness, much more fully available than we ever thought.

But the one in the wilderness does not see this. Although he received the Holy Spirit when God first saved him, he is still working on the flesh and finding it nothing but a wilderness. "Having begun in the Spirit," he is seeking to be "made perfect by the flesh," as Paul says in Galatians 3:3. More than that, he is living his Christian life largely under the law rather than under grace. It is not without significance that the wilderness where they wandered was called the desert of Sinai. Sinai was the place where the law was given, with its strict demands which we never seem able to meet. It tells us what we ought to do, but the flesh has no power to do it, and the law therefore cannot but condemn us. What a dry and thirsty place it is to live under its shadow, and that is invariably where we find ourselves living when we are not in Canaan. Charles Wesley understood this when he wrote in one of his great hymns:

> Oh, that I might at once go up,
> No more on this side Jordan stop,

> But now the land possess;
> This moment end my legal years,
> Sorrows and sins and doubts and fears,
> A howling wilderness.

We shall have something more to say in later pages about these "legal years."

To explain the wilderness experience we have had to go outside the Epistle to the Hebrews to other of Paul's writings. While we are doing this, there is one important passage we cannot ignore — 1 Corinthians 10:1-12. There Paul makes the point that whereas *all* the Israelites came out of Egypt and *all* were under the cloud and *all* passed through the sea and did *all* eat of the manna and drink of the rock that was smitten for them, with the great majority God was not well pleased, and they were overthrown in the wilderness.

LUST

He then goes on to say that in these things they became figures of ourselves and stresses the point that the very things that overthrew them in the wilderness may overthrow us there, too, and deprive us of our inheritance. He mentions five such things. The first is *lust*. "Now these things were our examples, to the intent that we should not lust after evil things as they also lusted." The reference here is to Numbers 11, where "the mixed multitude that was among them fell a-lusting: and the children of Israel also wept again and said, Who shall give us flesh to eat? We remember the fish which we did eat in Egypt for nought; and the cucumbers and the melons and the leeks and the onions and the garlic: but now our soul is dried away: there is nothing at all, beside this manna, before our eyes" (vv. 4-6).

In the Bible the word *lust* does not apply only to sex. Lust is a clamant desire that wants something and wants it now and is unsubordinated to the will of God. It is a wishing, wishing, wishing for what God has not given us. The fact that we do not have that thing means that, at the moment at least, it is not His will for us. Maybe He has it for us in the future, but we are not content to wait; we wish to have it now. Israel was wishing,

wishing, wishing for the melons and onions of Egypt. But God had not given them the melons and onions of Egypt: He had given them manna. And this lusting in their hearts made them lose their taste for that which God had given them — the precious, miraculous "bread of heaven." "There is nothing at all beside this manna before our eyes," they said; "Manna for breakfast, manna for dinner, and manna for supper!"

Who of us does not find himself wishing sometimes for what God has not given us; perhaps for a position God has not given us, or for possessions God has not given us, or for success God has not given us. For some it may be wishing, wishing for a husband God has not given, or for children God has not given, or for a better job God has not given. This wishing always makes us lose our taste for Jesus, the heavenly manna. We just cannot say truthfully that He is satisfying us when we have this lusting for something else in our hearts. In fact, we are not quite sure that we want Him to satisfy us; it is something else we want. The previous day we might have been in Canaan, but we have been indulging in this wishing and, as a result, we are in the wilderness. I believe we have to learn to repent of this sin of lust — wishing for what has not been given — and bring it to Jesus for forgiveness and cleansing if we are to find Him as all we need again. The manna was as "corriander seed and the colour like the colour of bdellium . . . and the taste of it was the taste of fresh oil." I don't know what all that means but obviously, even if it was not much to look at, it was mighty good to taste! We are certainly told that they could make cakes of it and doubtless there were all sorts of other attractive ways in which it could be served! But no, because of their lusting for what God had not given them, their soul "loathed this light bread."

The story ends with God granting them their request and giving them quail meat, but doing so on such a scale that it became obnoxious to them. "Ye shall not eat one day, nor two days, neither ten days, nor twenty days, but a whole month, till it come out at your nostrils and it be loathsome unto you." More than that, "While the flesh was between their teeth, 'ere it was chewed, the wrath of the Lord was kindled against the people, and the Lord smote the people with a very great plague." Thousands must have died in the epidemic that swept through the host and they were buried in a mass grave that came to be called, "The graves of lust," the English meaning of the Hebrew name they gave to it, Kabroth-hattaavah. The psalmist long after wrote a solemn epitaph over the whole incident in these words: "He gave them their request, but sent leanness into their soul," the latter phrase of which can be translated, thinned their numbers (106:15). Very often the worst thing God can give us is that which we have lusted after. It seldom works out suitably, it soon becomes obnoxious to us and ultimately brings us to misery; and over the ruins we have to put up the sign, as a sad testimonial, "The graves of lust." Be warned and repent of even the beginnings of this lusting, lest God give you your own way!

IDOLATRY

The second thing is *idolatry:* "Neither be ye idolaters as were some of them," referring to their worship of the golden calf. As people in Christ, we are meant to find all our interest and satisfaction in Him. We are, however, creatures of the world with various earthly needs, and God has promised to provide for them; but even when He does so, they are meant to be incidental to us and not our true life. But "God giveth us richly all things to enjoy," and this very generosity of His can create problems for us sometimes. These things can come to mean too much to us, our love of them can become inordinate, and they can take His place in our lives. Our idolatry takes various forms; it can be very close to that of Israel — worship of the golden calf. You do not necessarily have to have a lot of money to worship it. Indeed, those who do not have much money can love it and desire it more than those who have much of it. Paul elsewhere equates covetousness with idolatry: "covetousness which is idolatry," "a covetous man who is an idolater." Whenever I am worshiping anything or anyone more than Jesus, when I am not setting my mind on things above but on the things of earth to a degree more than God intends me to, that is idolatry; and if I do not know how to see it as sin and repent of it, I shall be overthrown in the wilderness. Inasmuch as we are, at least partly, creatures of earth and obviously must concentrate on many earthly concerns, only God can show us when our attitude has become idolatrous.

IMPURITY

The third thing is *impurity:* "Neither let us commit fornication as some of them committed and fell in one day three and twenty thousand." The reference here is to the incident in Numbers 25, where the children of Israel committed fornication with the daughters of Moab and as a result became involved in the sacrifices of their gods.

There is not one epistle of Paul in which he does not speak to the saints about sexual impurity of one sort or another. The Gentile society of that day was as corrupt and permissive as is ours today and what God was doing through the gospel was raising up a holy people out of the morass. He did not assume that every believer was completely out of it merely because he had professed conversion and had become part of the church. He knew that the believer could still be playing with these things.

We need the same word today. Even the most advanced believer is still in danger of this, sometimes in its grossest form, sometimes in its more subtle forms. And it can be subtle, especially with women. A man's temptations and failures along this line hit him hard and he knows them only too well, but good-living women sometimes find it difficult to identify this sin in themselves. I know of one woman who could never see this sin and repent of it until God showed her that she invariably acted very different when in the presence of men. When she was merely with women, she was "flat," but with men, she was so often a little kitten. Nothing more, but it was the same sin at the root, and she was able to take her place as a sinner at the cross of Jesus.

Paul, in this passage especially, nails the sin of fornication, as he does in his other epistles. I am sorry that the Revised Standard Version has always translated this word as "immorality." This is too diffuse a term and too relative. By that I mean that what one person regards as immoral, another person may not. And in this permissive age many people do not regard sexual relations outside of marriage as immoral or sinful. But Paul does and, infinitely more important, God does. God calls it fornication and He says we can be overthrown in the wilderness because of it.

On the other hand, the Revised Standard Version does us a service in another place (1 Cor. 6:9) by substituting the one word *homosexuals* for the two old English expressions, *effeminate* and *abusers of themselves with mankind*, so that the verse reads: "Be not deceived . . . homosexuals shall not inherit the kingdom of God," nor will a number of other categories of sinners, as the complete verse makes clear (I have quoted only part of it). I remember a young man coming to me one day in great distress, pointing to this verse and this word *homosexuals*. "This is my trouble," he said, "and it says I cannot inherit the kingdom of God." How glad I was to be able to point to the message of grace and mercy in the next verse: "And such were some of you, but ye are washed, ye are sanctified, ye are justified in the name of the Lord Jesus and by the Spirit of our God." Even such can get out of the wilderness into the land of milk and honey by the complete cleansing of the all-availing blood of Jesus, which will be the theme of later chapters.

TEMPTING THE LORD

The fourth thing is *tempting the Lord:* "Neither let us tempt the Lord, as some of them tempted and were destroyed of serpents." Tempting the Lord was one of Israel's most persistent sins in the wilderness, though only the incident in Numbers 21 is referred to here. Psalm 95, from which Paul quotes so fully in Hebrews 3, describes their whole sojourn in the desert as a "day of temptation in the wilderness, when your fathers tempted me by proving me and saw my works forty years." In another psalm, Psalm 78, which gives a review of Israel's behavior from Egypt to Canaan, we have this word about tempting the Lord three times: "They tempted God in their hearts by asking meat for their lust . . . they turned back and tempted God and limited the Holy One of Israel . . . they tempted and provoked the most high God and kept not his statutes." And in Numbers 14, when at Kadesh-Barnea the people refused to go into the land, the Lord complained, "All those men . . . have tempted me now these ten times." And it is always spoken of as something that provoked the Lord to anger, involving them in grievous disciplines and losses.

What an extraordinary phrase, to tempt the Lord! We can understand about man being tempted but how can God be tempted, and that by us? Apparently it is possible, because Jesus rejected Satan's proposition to throw Himself down from the temple by saying that such action would be to tempt God, and to do so was forbidden. As Dr. Packer defines it, "Man tempts God by attitudes, words or behaviour which in effect constitute a defiant challenge to Him to prove the truth of His words and the goodness and justice of His ways." And Israel did just that under the tests God allowed to come upon them. When they lacked water, they argued with Moses and said, "Is the Lord among us or not?" They doubted whether He was with them and in effect they challenged Him to prove it. On another occasion, "they tempted God in their hearts, by asking meat for their lust . . . they said, Can God furnish a table in the wilderness?" (Ps. 78:18,19). That was not a question asked in faith but a complaint that He had not done so and an expression of doubt as to whether He could or would. And this attitude on their part constituted a temptation to God — it tempted God to deal with them according to their unbelief and live up to (or should we say, live down to) their low thoughts of Him, i.e., to forsake them and spread no table for them in the wilderness. Had He done so, no one could have charged Him with injustice. But, being merciful and gracious, He did not do it, but provided what He had already been planning for them. But what a grievous provocation of Him it was! So grievous indeed, that He disciplined them, in the case quoted here, by sending a great invasion of venomous snakes among them and there was a further thinning of their numbers in the wilderness.

In the same way, we too have tempted God when we have been tested. We have doubted His guidance and provision and have asked the same querulous questions that Israel did: "If He is with me, how can He have allowed me to be in this fix? Don't talk to me about trusting Him now; how can He furnish a table in a wilderness like this?" William Cowper, who went through so many deep trials in his life, wrote:

> Judge not the Lord by feeble sense,
>   But trust Him for His grace;
> Behind a frowning providence
>   He hides a smiling face.

But we do judge the Lord by feeble sense. We do not trust Him for His grace; all we imagine we see is a frowning providence and we miss the sight of that smiling face. Did you know that such attitudes of unbelief are a temptation to God? He says, "You are tempting me to act as if I was not with you and as if I was not going to provide a table in the wilderness." Of course, He resists the temptation. He does not change His mind regarding us. But He disciplines us for our attitude, nonetheless, and we find ourselves overthrown in the wilderness, that is, deprived of the fullness of His blessing, if nothing more. Who of us has not, in the hour of trial, "tempted God in the desert" again and again and chosen to believe the worst? But have we begun to see this as a grievous provocation of God and to repent of it as sin? God gives us every encouragement to do so, because grace is there to bring the erring one again into the Promised Land.

MURMURING

The fifth thing that overthrew them in the wilderness was *murmuring:* "Neither murmur ye, as some of them also murmured and were destroyed of the destroyer." This was another of their frequent sins in the wilderness and I believe it is ours too. It is simply complaining about what God has allowed; and, be assured, if it has happened, it is because God has allowed it — there are no second causes — and to complain is virtually to rebel against God. Furthermore, it invariably leads us to blame others. If we cannot blame God directly, then we blame somebody else; and how unhappy this makes those we are blaming. Sometimes it is those at home who are made to feel the weight of our blame; sometimes it is the leader God has given us (perhaps our minister) that we are criticizing, as Israel did. But Moses had to say to them: "What are Aaron and I? Your murmurings are not against us, but against the Lord."

Such murmuring is no light matter in the eyes of God, seen by the fact that those involved were "destroyed by the destroyer" and further loss of life was involved. If the Lord Jesus is to bring us up out of the wilderness, we will have to judge this before Him as the sin it is; and we will do that only as we see that our murmurings have not been against man but against God, who has allowed things the way they are, and that for wise purposes of His own. Perhaps the wise purpose may simply be to teach us new lessons of submission to Him and patience, and we just have not been willing to learn them.

What a story this is, that of Israel in the wilderness! It is a narrative of one long provocation of Jehovah. I have noted no less than thirteen such provocations, beginning with their reaction to Jehovah's first proposition to deliver them from Egypt, right on through the wilderness to the death of Moses. At each test it was the same thing. All of them brought grief to the One who had redeemed them from their bondage and longed to bring them into the new land He had promised, and nearly all brought severe chastenings on themselves. Little wonder that He complained, "They do alway err in their heart, and they have not known my ways"; and little wonder that He ultimately sware in His wrath that they should not enter into His rest.

As each one of us looks over our own course "from Egypt until now" and at our many similar provocations of the Lord, let us confess that He is right to swear in His wrath that we should not enter into His rest. Nothing is more important than this attitude of brokenness that says, "O God, Thou art right and I am wrong," because, having humbled ourselves in this way before Him, it is our privilege to pray the great revival prayer in Habbakuk 3:2: "In wrath remember mercy." This is the prayer of the penitent and one that God cannot fail to answer, for "He delighteth in mercy." As someone has said, "Mercy is God's weak point," and whoever touches Him there receives an answer exceeding abundantly above all that he asked or thought.

Then there is found the way out of all this shadow Christian life into the substance. Jesus and His blood are the way out of every wilderness into which our sin gets us. He is not only our Canaan, but the easily accessible way into it. When the children of that first generation did eventually enter Canaan under Joshua, the ark of the covenant, borne on the shoulders of the priests, went first into the river Jordan. Upon the mercy seat, which topped the ark, were the blood stains of the annual sacrifice, which had been sprinkled upon it. As the priests' feet touched the river, the waters parted, and they stood in the Jordan, bearing the ark, until the people were clean passed over. The Jordan that seems to bar your entrance into rest is still parted, for His blood still avails. Come to Him again, then, as a sinner on the points at issue, first with regard to the works of the flesh that have been apparent and then the enthronement of self as the cause of it all, and you will find that by the power of His blood He so forgives and cleanses you as to bring you from the weary wilderness to find your all in Him.

As we close the theme of going on from the wilderness into the Promised Land, let us use the same urgent words that Paul uses in closing this aspect. Here we have two other verses that begin with "Let us." "Let us therefore fear lest, a promise being left us of entering into his rest, any of you should seem to come short of it" (4:1). How pathetic it would be if we stopped short of that which is so greatly needed and so clearly promised — entering into His rest, or, as alternatively phrased, being made a partaker of Christ. It is the pathos of a situation in which a valuable inheritance is left a beneficiary in a will, but that beneficiary never comes forward to claim it. Efforts are made to trace him, advertisements are inserted in newspapers, saying that if he will apply to a certain firm of solicitors, "he will hear something to his advantage." But he never shows up in order to partake of his inheritance. Oh, the sadness of the promise being left us of entering into His rest and we never claiming it and entering in.

Paul's further word of exhortation in the matter is this: "Let us labour therefore to enter into that rest, lest any man fall after the same example of unbelief" or disobedience (4:11). Here we have the pathos of not simply failing to enter into what is promised, but rather of being overthrown in the wilderness and remaining overthrown. To be told to labor to enter into rest may sound like a contradiction in terms, but it is put in this way to emphasize that the Christian is to make entering into God's rest his number-one priority and to let nothing stand in the way of his doing so.

On the other hand, we must understand that this entering into Canaan is not necessarily a once-for-all experience. At any moment the voice of God may come to us, "Ye have compassed this mountain long enough; turn you northward" (Deut. 2:3), and we wake up to realize that we have gone back to compassing Mount Sinai again, mourning over ourselves, and are in the wilderness once more. But Jesus, our Canaan, is still there for us and the way into that Canaan, His powerful blood, is still available to us, no matter in what new state of need we feel ourselves to be. The Christian life is really simply a matter of facing up continually as to where we are content to dwell — in the wilderness or in Canaan. If nothing but Canaan will satisfy us, then that is all the time available to us and on the easiest possible terms. So today, let us go on from living in the wilderness to living in Canaan.

Let Us Go On

From Knowing Jesus as Our Aaron to Knowing Him as Our Melchizedek

Thou art a priest for ever after the order of Melchizedek . . .

. . . even Jesus, made an high priest for ever after the order of Melchizedek.

For this Melchizedek, king of Salem, priest of the most high God, who met Abraham returning from the slaughter of the kings, and blessed him, to whom also Abraham gave a tenth part of all; first being by interpretation king of righteousness, and after that also king of Salem, which is king of peace; without father, without mother, without genealogy, having neither beginning of days, nor end of life, but made like unto the Son of God, continues a priest for ever.

Now consider how great this man was, unto whom even the patriarch Abraham gave the tenth of the spoils. And verily they that are of the sons of Levi, who receive the office of the priesthood, have a commandment to take tithes of the people according to the law, that is, of their brethren though they come out of the loins of Abraham; but he whose genealogy is not counted from them received tithes of Abraham, and blessed him that had the promises. And without all contradiction the less is blessed of the better. And here men that die receive tithes; but there he receiveth them, of whom it is testified that he liveth. And as I may so say, Levi also, who receiveth tithes, paid tithes in Abraham; for he was yet in the loins of his father, when Melchizedek met him.

If therefore perfection were by the Levitical priesthood (for under it the people received the law), what further need was there that another priest should rise after the order of Melchizedek and not be called after the order of Aaron? For the priesthood being changed, there is made of necessity a change also of the law. For he of whom these things are spoken pertaineth to another tribe, of which no man gave attendance at the altar. For it is evident that our Lord sprang out of Judah, of which tribe Moses spake nothing concerning priesthood. And this becomes even more evident when another priest arises after the likeness of Melchizedek who has become a priest, not after the law of a carnal commandment, but after the power of an endless life. For he testifieth, Thou art a priest for ever after the order of Melchizedek.

For there is verily a disannulling of the commandment going before for the weakness and unprofitableness thereof (for the law made nothing perfect), and a bringing in thereupon of a better hope, through which we draw nigh unto God.

And inasmuch as not without an oath he was made priest; (for those priests were made without an oath; but this with an oath by him that said unto him, the Lord sware and will not repent, Thou art a priest forever after the order of Melchizedek) by so much was Jesus made a surety of a better testament.

And they truly were many priests, because they were not suffered to continue by reason of death;

but this man, because he continueth ever, hath an unchangeable priesthood. Wherefore he is able also to save them to the uttermost that come unto God by him, seeing he ever liveth to make intercession for them.

For such a high priest became us, who is holy, harmless, undefiled, separate from sinners, and made higher than the heavens; who needeth not daily, as those high priests, to offer up sacrifice, first for his own sins and then for the people's;

for this he did once when he offered up himself.

For the law maketh men high priests which have infirmity; but the word of the oath which was after the law appointeth the Son, who is consecrated for evermore.

— Hebrews 5:6; 6:20; 7:1-28

3

Let Us Go On

From Knowing Jesus as Our Aaron to Knowing Him as Our Melchizedek

WE COME NOW to the very heart of what Paul has to say — that Jesus is a high priest after the order of Melchizedek. After his very first allusion to Melchizedek, he says, "Of whom we have many things to say." Then he proceeds to say these things, and they occupy a large portion of the great epistle. He goes on to say they are "hard to be understood, seeing ye are become dull of hearing." I do not think they are really hard to understand — quite simple, in fact — unless of course we have become dull of hearing, that is, spiritually ignorant. And remember, a state of ignorance comes about through a continual ignoring of what God is saying to us and is therefore something culpable in the Christian life. That is why Paul uses the phrase "and are *become* dull of hearing." But if our hearts are hungry and open to God's voice, either in conviction or in encouragement, there is nothing very complicated here. It is the same simple message of the grace of God with which we began our Christian lives and which we must "hold steadfast to the end." So don't be put off by the high-sounding name of Melchizedek. It is just a name like John or Robert, which we give to our children — though I don't think your son would thank you if he had to go through life called Melchizedek!

Very soon in this epistle Paul introduces the thought that just as God provided for His ancient people a high priest, so He has provided for us the spiritual counterpart of one in the Lord Jesus. He brings before us two priesthoods, one after the order of Aaron and the other after the order of Melchizedek. Who and what Melchizedek was we shall see in a moment. The great point he makes is that the order of Melchizedek was clearly superior to that of Aaron and superseded it. As we shall see, both these priests are types and foreshadowings of the Lord Jesus. Therefore, inasmuch as Melchizedek is greater than Aaron, it is obvious that what the former typifies of Christ must be greater than what the latter does. And the question we want to ask ourselves in this chapter is, Have we entered into that which Melchizedek typifies of Christ or do we know only that which Aaron typifies? Paul urges us to go on from knowing Jesus as our Aaron to knowing Him as our Melchizedek.

Let us start with Aaron and his priesthood, which is the first type of Christ in this epistle.

A high priest is "ordained for men in things pertaining to God," says Paul. As a people in a special relationship to God, they needed a representative before Him, someone who would take care on their behalf of all matters connected with that relationship. It was a serious thing for Israel if they got wrong with God; all their prosperity and all their defense against their enemies depended on that relationship. They needed someone who knew how to maintain it continually for them and restore it when it got broken. That was the function of a high priest and God provided them one in Aaron.

This is precisely the office the Lord Jesus fills for the saints today. All the way through this epistle we have Him presented to us as our High Priest, taking care of our relationship with God, on which everything for us depends, maintaining it for us and restoring it when it goes wrong. When at the beginning of chapter 8 Paul pauses to summarize how far he has got, he says, "Now of the things which we have spoken, this is the sum: We have such an high priest, who is set on the right hand of the Majesty in the heavens, a minister of the sanctuary, and of the true tabernacle which the Lord pitched, and not man."

THREE QUALIFICATIONS

According to this epistle, a high priest had to have three qualifications for this holy office. First, he had to be chosen from among men. "For every high priest taken from among men is ordained for men in things pertaining to God . . . who can bear gently with the ignorant and erring, for that he himself also is compassed with infirmity" (5:1,2). He who was to represent man before God had to be man himself, compassed with the same weaknesses as those he represented and therefore able to bear gently with their infirmities and have compassion for their failings and mistakes. Such was Aaron, himself one of the people whom he was called to represent before God.

And such is the Lord Jesus. The One who in the first chapter is shown as the unique Son of God, heir of all things, the brightness of God's glory, the express image of His person, upholding all things by the word of His power, is seen in the second chapter as stooping to be "made like unto his brethren in all things." He who is "made better than the angels as he hath obtained a more excellent name than they" is seen in that second chapter as being made lower than those angels, not taking upon Himself their nature but going lower to take on Him the seed of Abraham. "Forasmuch as the children are partakers of flesh and blood, he also took part of the same" (2:14). We see Him there as a Brother among brethren (2:12a), a Worshiper among worshipers (2:12b), a Believer among believers (3:13a), and a Child among children (3:13b). God has arranged it that in every conceivable way Jesus has been made like unto His brethren. There are only two matters in which He is not like them — His virgin birth and His sinless life. But in everything else, He has been identified with them in their infirmities. There are no sufferings that His brethren suffer but that He has suffered them too. No poverty-stricken man of earth can go to Jesus and say, "I am poorer than You were." As St. Francis used to say, "Jesus was married to Lady Poverty." He had nowhere to lay His head; today He would have slept under the arches. There are no tears that His brethren shed, but that He has shed them too. Indeed, He is described in this very epistle as "offering up prayers and supplications with strong crying and tears unto him that was able to save him from death"; and He was not delivered but had to go through with it. There are no deprivation of rights, no indignities that His brethren suffer but He suffered them too — in Pilate's judgment hall and on the cross, where He was numbered with the transgressors and classed by everyone as such, when He was not one at all. God has made the Captain of our salvation perfect through suffering. He would not be an adequate High Priest for us had He not been through everything that we go through.

His Name is Jesus, He is my Friend
He is human as well as divine;
I want you to meet Him, I want you
to greet Him,
This wonderful Saviour of mine.

Yes, Jesus is human, as well as divine; in the heavenly glory He wears our humanity still; He is still the Son of man, which means He is never untouched with the feeling of our weaknesses. In our hour of suffering He says, "Come to Me, all you who labor and are heavy laden. I am your Brother, I have been made like unto you in everything." I was much touched to read an incident regarding the death of Princess Elizabeth, a daughter of King Charles I, who was beheaded at Whitehall, London. She was cast into prison, where she contracted tuberculosis and died, sad and neglected. When they found her, her Bible was open, her head lying on this very text, "Come unto me all ye that labour and are heavy laden, and I will give you rest" (Matt. 11:28). The historian at this point added a little sentence: "She found comfort in the One who, as her Brother, was made like unto her in all things." Only so is Jesus qualified to be our Aaron.

There was a second qualification for a high priest — he had to have something to offer. Minutely described in the Book of Leviticus is a whole range of sacrifices and offerings which the high priest had to offer to God on behalf of the people. "Wherefore it is of necessity that this man have somewhat also to offer," says Paul (8:3). What has this Man, Jesus, to offer? He offered Himself. All the offerings of the Old Testament were but foreshadowings and types of this offering. Nothing less would atone for sin and put man back into relationship with God. "When he had by himself purged our sins. . . .This he did once when he offered up himself. . . ." No other offering would do, so great is human guilt before God. He is not only the Offerer but the Offering.

I am thinking of Isaac, as he went up Mount Moriah with Abraham to offer a burnt offering to God. He had often helped his father offer sacrifices. They usually brought a lamb with them for a burnt offering, or perhaps they would find a wild goat on the hill — and he expected the same to happen this time. A bit puzzled, he says to his father, "We've got the fire and we've got the wood but where is the lamb for the burnt offering?" I think Abraham answered with broken voice, "It is going to be you this time." And that is what the Father said to the Son. There had been many lambs slain all down the centuries, but one day He said, "It is going to be You this time." Only so could the Lord Jesus be our high priest and deliver us from the power of our great enemy, Satan. His partaking of our flesh and blood was not merely that He might be made like His brethren in all things and therefore able to sympathize with them in their infirmities, but supremely that "through death he might destroy him that had the power of death . . . and deliver them who through fear of death were all their lifetime subject to bondage" (2:14,15).

The third qualification of a high priest was that he must not be self-appointed, but called of God. "No man taketh this honour unto himself, but he that is called of God, as was Aaron" (5:4). It was just so with the Lord Jesus; He "glorified not himself to be made an high priest, but he that said unto him, Thou art my Son. . . . Thou art a priest . . . " (5:5,6). It was not He who appointed Himself as our high priest, but the Father. It was the Father who said to Him, "You are to be their high priest." That comforts me. I would have thought that God would blame me for my failures, that He would be the One with the big stick. Instead of this, I see Him in His mercy providing a high priest for a sinner like me. Here one of the basic truths of the gospel shines through — that God is for men, not against them. And Jesus on His part is going to be "faithful to him that appointed him" (3:2) — not faithful to me so much as faithful to God. That is what is meant by the expression Paul uses here, "a merciful and faithful high priest" — merciful to me but faithful to God. He is never going to fall down on the job the Father has given Him to do, that of taking care of the interests of the feeblest saints before His face. No matter how failing they may feel themselves to be, no matter how disappointed in themselves they may become, they will never fail to find a "Friend at court" to represent them, someone to whom they can go in every time of need just as they are. The Father has arranged it that way. My peace with God, then, does not depend on my faithfulness to God; it does not even depend on Christ's faithfulness to me, but rather on Christ's faithfulness to Him who has appointed Him for me. What a pillow to rest the head on!

A FURTHER FULLNESS

So it is we see Jesus as our Aaron and can know Him as such. You may ask, "Is it possible for Him to mean more to us that this? — it is all so gloriously positive!" He can indeed mean more than this and the apostle is concerned to show us a further fullness in the Lord Jesus by proving from the Old Testament prophecies that the Father had actually appointed Him a priest after another order from that of Aaron, and an infinitely superior one. Paul comes to this by way of meeting an objection that would obviously be in the minds of his Hebrew readers. Having heard what he had said of Jesus as our high priest, they might well have said, "We already have a high priest. Aaron and his descendants were appointed by God Himself and one of them is even now occupying that office. Do we need another one? Would God who has appointed us one high priest then appoint another?"

In answering this objection, Paul comes to the main theme of this epistle which lights up the fullness in the Lord Jesus for us even further.

He reminds them of the great Psalm 110, which every Jew admitted to be messianic, that is, prophetic of the Messiah. It begins with David saying, "Jehovah saith unto my Lord, Sit thou on my right hand until I make thine enemies thy footstool." Paul reminds the Hebrews that one verse in that psalm says, "Jehovah hath sworn and will not repent, Thou art a priest for ever after the order of Melchizedek." The Messiah apparently is not to be a priest after the order of Aaron, but after the order of Melchizedek. That in turn would take his readers back to Genesis 14, where Melchizedek appears for one fleeting moment on the page of history. Abraham has come back from a victorious battle and is met by this man who is distinctly said to be "the priest of the most high God." It is extraordinary that amidst the universal paganism of those days, before the Law was given, there should be this "priest of the most high God." Where he has come from we are not told. No genealogy of him is given (and how important a priest's genealogy was in Old Testament times) and there is no record of his death. Paul says in effect, for all we know he might be living forever; he is "without father, without mother, without genealogy, having neither beginning of days nor end of life." It does not take much spiritual insight to see that he can well be taken as a type and foreshadowing of the Lord Jesus.

The interesting thing is that Melchizedek assumed a place of superiority over Abraham in that he blessed him saying, "Blessed be Abram of the most high God, possessor of heaven and earth," and, as Paul points out, "Without all contradiction the less is blessed of the better" (7:7). Abraham, on his part, acknowledged his superiority in that he gave him tithes of all the spoil. From this, Paul makes the point that inasmuch as Levi and Aaron were yet in the loins of their ancestor when Melchizedek met him, they were in effect paying him tithes in Abraham. They who were later ordained to receive tithes from the people were paying them to Melchizedek and thus acknowledging the superiority of his priesthood over their own.

The Bible reader would pass over this incident in Genesis 14 as of little importance but for the fact that David, centuries after, makes a definite allusion to it as being prophetic of the Messiah's priesthood, and Paul in his epistle makes it the pivot around which he builds his message that the Lord Jesus is a priest of a superior order to that of Aaron.

If Aaron is in so many ways a type of Christ, it must be that Melchizedek gives us an even fuller picture of Him. In what way does Melchizedek picture a fuller provision for us in Jesus? That is the matter we now seek to explore.

Paul makes great play on this Scripture, "The Lord sware and will not repent, Thou art a priest for ever after the order of Melchizedek." He quotes it no fewer than four times and on each occasion he emphasizes a different part of the verse. The first time he quotes it is in 5:6 and here the emphasis is on *"Thou art,"* showing that Christ glorified not Himself to be made a high priest, but that He became such by the call and appointment of God. We have already seen this when we were thinking of Jesus as our Aaron and we saw the comfort and encouragement that that was meant to be to us. Jesus, in being our Melchizedek, does not cease to be our Aaron. He is all that is pictured by Aaron, but more, as we shall see, and is certainly called of God to that high office.

The second time he quotes the verse is in 6:20 and the emphasis there is on these words: *"a priest after the order of Melchizedek."* We have just summarized his arguments in which he shows that this means that His is a priesthood of an infinitely superior order to that of Aaron.

"A PRIEST FOR EVER"

The third place where this verse is quoted is in 7:17 and here the emphasis (and this is the most important one) is on the words "a priest *for ever.*" In contrast to the old order of high priests, none of whom continued because of death, this Man is alive, and that forever. He has neither "beginning of days nor end of life" and therefore abides a priest continually. His priestly ministry for us (and we shall see what that is in a moment) is continuous and unchanging. Whatever Jesus is to us, He is that *all the time.*

The most important contrast, however, between the old order of priests and this Man is that whereas their ministry was on earth, His is in heaven and continues right now. Indeed, Paul says that if He were on earth, He would not be a priest at all, because there were still in those days remnants of that old order offering gifts according to the law (8:4). But Jesus is exercising His ministry for us in heaven. As our Melchizedek, He has "not entered into the holy place made with hands, which are the figures of the true, but into heaven itself, now to appear in the presence of God for us" (9:24); and that heavenly high priesthood of Christ, rightly understood, is something we need more than anything else.

What then, is He doing for us in heaven? Paul says He is there "ever living to make intercession for us," because of which He can impart a continual and contemporary salvation to all that come to God by Him (7:25). It is of first importance that we should understand what this phrase "Jesus making intercession for us" means, for our experience must be based on understood truth.

We must understand that what is in view here is the matter of guilt and that it constitutes a continual need in the lives of the saints. They have not finished with the problem of guilt just because they have put an initial faith in Christ. The guilt of all that has happened up to that moment is certainly expunged and they are assured forever of their position as children of God. But subsequent failures and sins all leave their legacy of guilt; and the guilt that we incur before God is reflected by a corresponding sense of guilt in our hearts and we lose our peace, our joy, our sense of triumphing, and we know that things are not right between us and God. It is not suggested here that the saint who has sinned loses his place in the family of God, but he certainly loses his fellowship with his heavenly Father. And to the one who knows the reality and sweetness of that fellowship, that is a grievous loss indeed.

The fact is that the saints are experiencing some sort of guilt in their hearts almost daily. If it is not a condemning heart because of some infringement of the divine law of, say, love to our neighbor, it is a sense of guilt by seeing another's devotion to Christ. To hear, for instance, of how long another person spends in prayer can often have the effect of giving us a sense of guilt because we have not been doing the same. Again and again it is coming to us from one quarter or another, sometimes a true guilt, sometimes a false guilt, but guilt nonetheless, as far as our experience is concerned. Our hearts are often like a sunlit field of grain on which shadows of clouds are chasing themselves across that otherwise sunny expanse. The area of guilt is Satan's chosen field of operations. He is called in Scripture the "accuser of the brethren, who accuses them before their God day and night" (Rev. 12:10) — and not only before their God, but to their own hearts as well. By the way he accuses them of their failures and shortcomings, one might almost think that he was a holiness preacher! Nothing of the sort, of course; his purpose is to give the saints an experience of guilt again and who can tell what loss and damage in their daily relationship to God they experience as a result? Did they but know it, the element of guilt constitutes one of their basic and continuous problems.

The whole context of this epistle makes it clear that it is the matter of the guilt and the defilement of the saints which is the subject of the continuous intercession of Christ in heaven. That this is so is further confirmed if you look at Romans 8:34 where Christ's present intercession for us is also mentioned. Paul asks "Who is he that condemneth? Shall Christ Jesus that died . . . who is even at the right hand of God, who also maketh intercession for us?" The answer to that question is that He is obviously not condemning us, because it is concerning the very matter of our guilt that He is making intercession for us in heaven. He is there not as the counsel for the prosecution, but for our defense.

If that is the matter He is dealing with, how does His intercession for us answer it? I do not think this phrase means that He is praying to the Father for us in the sense that one of us might pray for another. It is something infinitely more than His beseeching God to be gracious to us. *The mere fact that He is in heaven at all is His intercession for us.* It is an utter marvel that He was ever able to go back to heaven, after accepting responsibility for all the sins of the world on the cross. He had on Him more sins than any other man. A man can bear only his own sins; He bore the world's. As an old hymn says, "He made them His very own." How can such an One as He, with all the sins of the world, go back into heaven? What excludes the sinner must also exclude his Surety. But Paul tells us, *"By his own blood* he entered in once for all into the holy place, having obtained eternal redemption for us" (9:12). Not even Jesus could get into that heavenly place in any other way than by His blood. Indeed, in another place we are told it was only by that blood that He was brought again from the dead (13:20). The everlasting doors which had barred access to all sinners lifted up their heads and let the King of Glory in when He came presenting His own blood. That blood declared He had fully exhausted the judgment of all the sins for which He had accepted responsibility and therefore He was received in. If that blood was enough to bring Him again from the dead and into the Holiest, it is certainly enough for me. The mere fact that He is in heaven at all today is proof that His judgment-bearing on Calvary is enough and that there is "power, wonder-working power in the blood of the Lamb." I say again, if the blood that He shed was enough to bring Him into heaven after being made a terrible effigy of sin on the cross, it is certainly enough to give me peace with regard to my particular sins and bring me into fellowship with God.

This, then, is His intercession for me as an erring, failing saint. All the time there He is in heaven before the face of God as an answer for my sin. Without saying a word, His wounds are His constant intercession for me in the hour when Satan accuses and a sense of guilt lies upon my spirit.

When Satan tempts me to despair
And tells me of the guilt within,
Upward I look and see Him there,
Who made an end of all my sin.

My name is graven on His hands,
My name is written on His heart,
I know that while in heaven He stands,
No tongue can bid me thence depart.

This does not rule out that there may be many a conversation between the Son and the Father regarding me, His needy child, but the basis of the intercession of my heavenly Melchizedek is always His blood.

This fact is caught by many of our precious gospel hymns,

only the word used is often "plead" rather than "make interces-sion."

> At the blest Mercy Seat
> Pleading for me,
> My feeble faith looks up,
> Jesus, to Thee.

Pleading there does not mean wringing His hands and be-seeching God on our behalf. It is, rather, a legal term. It is the picture of an advocate in a court of law, "pleading" on behalf of his client, that is, bringing a plea in the form of evidence on the grounds of which he expects him to be acquitted. And Jesus is doing this all the time for us; but for this, our relationship with God would long since have become null and void. And His plea for us is ever His blood.

> Five bleeding wounds He bears
> Received on Calvary,
> They pour effectual prayers,
> They strongly plead for me:
> Forgive him, O forgive, they cry,
> Nor let that ransomed sinner die.

The result of His intercession for me is that I may know a continual, contemporary salvation. "Wherefore he is able to save them to the uttermost [margin, evermore] them that come unto God by him" (7:25). That salvation is twofold. First, I may know a continual cleansing from the guilt and defilement of sin as it may occur. Not only does the blood of Jesus speak for me in heaven, but it cleanses my heart on earth as I am willing to call sin, sin, and to repent, and nothing is a greater inducement to such honesty and brokenness than the knowl-edge that the worst as well as the least has been anticipated and settled in that precious blood which He presents before the Father.

This continual salvation also includes something else. Down from my High Priest in heaven comes a continual supply of His own life. Imagine a diver at the bottom of the sea and suppose we could go and talk to him. We say, "How can you live down here, surrounded by water?"

He says, "I've got a friend up there, and there is a tube

between him and me. But for him, I would die in a moment."

So we go up to the top to have a look at this friend. In a boat we see a man turning a handle (in the old days, before they did these things by electricity). He says, "Don't disturb me; I've got to turn this handle."

We say, "Can't you stop and have a little picnic?"

He says, "No, I've got a friend down there and he is utterly dependent on me. Just as long as he is down there, I've got to turn this handle."

You and I have a Friend up there, a heavenly High Priest who never ceases to make intercession for us. All the time He is presenting the value of that once-for-all sacrifice. But for Him, I would die in a moment; but if I keep coming to God by Him in my need, He sends His resurrection life down into my heart and I live, "yet not I, but Christ liveth in me." And I find I can live in this sinful world with everything opposing me. People cannot understand it. But my answer is "I've got a Friend up there, and by His Holy Spirit I am linked to Him and I share in His own life." And so we can sing:

> By His death and endless life,
> Jesus saves.

"THE LORD SWARE"

We have yet to look at the fourth place where this great prophecy of Psalm 110 is quoted. It is in Hebrews 7:21, where the emphasis is on the words *"The Lord sware and will not repent."* Here we have the immutability of the grace of God. It "alters not when it alteration finds." The Lord has sworn that His people are going to have a heavenly high priest, and no matter how needy and failing they may be, nor how disappointed in themselves they may feel, He is not going to repent of it, that is, change His mind. Paul makes the point that the old order of priests was made "without an oath; but this one . . . with an oath" (7:21), and an oath which God will never go back on. Their weaknesses and failures will not alter His appointment of a high priest for them, because the very nature of His priesthood has taken account of all these things even before they have taken place. The value of His blood is the whole content of His intercession. Not only *will* He never repent of this provision, but there is no *need* that He should; for, our High Priest has anticipated and settled by His work on the cross the very things that the needy saint sometimes feels must surely make God give him up. And it is that settlement which Jesus is constantly presenting in the presence of God for him.

What hope these words "The Lord sware and will not repent . . ." give to the hesitant soul. He need not despair, but come boldly to the throne of grace to obtain mercy and find grace to help in every time of need. Paul says in 6:19 that this hope is an anchor of the soul, both sure and steadfast. Ships are normally anchored down; the believer, however, is anchored up, for this verse goes on to say that this anchor "entereth into that within the veil, whither the forerunner is for us entered, even Jesus, made an high priest after the order of Melchizedek."

The men of the world are anchored down, hoping to find their peace and security in the things of the earth. There is a story of a small boat which had anchored off shore at low tide, while its occupants fished. As the tide came in, there was an increasing strain upon the cable of the anchor. When, however, they sought to lift the anchor they found they could not. It was inextricably caught and defied all their attempts to lift it, and they had no means by which to break the iron cable, which ultimately dragged them all down to their death in the rising tide. What a solemn picture of the inevitable end of the "men of the world who have their portion in this life," anchored down to that which will ultimately destroy them. Not so the child of God who has this hope in Jesus within the veil. He is anchored up and can truly sing:

> When darkness seems to hide His face,
> I rest on His unchanging grace;
> In ev'ry high and stormy gale,
> My anchor holds within the veil.

Are we now able to discern the difference between knowing Jesus as our Aaron and knowing Him as our Melchizedek? When we know Him only as our Aaron, we look back to His work for us on earth, back to His cross. And it is never wrong so to do. What can be more spiritually moving than that backward look, as expressed sometimes in our greatest hymns?

> My soul looks back to see
> The burdens Thou did'st bear,
> When hanging on th' accursed tree
> And knows her guilt was there.

The trouble, however, is that that is all we may see in the Lord Jesus, and this in turn means that we tend to look back only to our conversion. When we sing gospel hymns of testimony, it is so often only of our conversion we are thinking and we try to recapture that first glow. We are inclined to think that the more heartily we sing, "O happy day, when Jesus washed my sins away," the more likely we are to feel again the joys of that first release. Our testimony is perhaps many years old; we have nothing fresh to tell; we have not an up-to-date sinner's testimony. This is basically due to the fact that we have not been "walking in the light" (1 John 1:7), that is, being honest about our present needs and sins and seeing in Jesus the ever-present answer.

When, however, we are knowing Jesus as our Melchizedek, we are not looking back to Calvary, but up to Calvary, where we see an ever-living Savior in the presence of God for us as the answer to every sin and accusation, who is sending down to us every conceivable grace to help in time of need. This means that we can afford to be real and honest and call sin, sin; the pressure is off us to pretend we are better than we are; and as a result, we know many sweet deliverances of grace, and our testimony to Jesus becomes gloriously up-to-date.

Let us go on, then, from knowing Jesus as our Aaron to knowing Him as our Melchizedek. Let us move on from a testimony that is, perhaps, many years old to something contemporary and up-to-date. That can happen only as we come with our needs which are up-to-date, and our sins which are up-to-date. Perhaps something went wrong yesterday and we have not come to Jesus with it. But when we do, we will find we have a heavenly Savior who is gloriously up-to-date.

Let Us Go On

From Living Under the Old Covenant to Living Under the New

But now hath he obtained a more excellent ministry, by how much also he is the mediator of a better covenant, which was established upon better promises. For if that first covenant had been faultless, then should no place have been sought for the second. For finding fault with it, He saith,

> Behold, the days come, saith the Lord, when I will make a new covenant with the house of Israel and with the house of Judah: not according to the covenant that I made with their fathers in the day when I took them by the hand to lead them out of the land of Egypt; because they continued not in my covenant, and I regarded them not, saith the Lord.

> For this is the covenant that I will make with the house of Israel after those days, saith the Lord; I will put my laws into their mind, and write them in their hearts: and I will be to them a God, and they shall be to me a people; and they shall not teach every man his neighbour, and every man his brother, saying, Know the Lord; for all shall know me, from the least to the greatest. For I will be merciful to their unrighteousness, and their sins and their iniquities will I remember no more.

In that he saith, A new covenant, he hath made the first old [RSV, obsolete]. Now that which decayeth [RSV, what is become obsolete] and waxeth old is ready to vanish away.

— Hebrews 8:6-13

4

Let Us Go On

From Living Under the Old Covenant to Living Under the New

THE FACT THAT it was prophesied that a priest should arise after the order of Melchizedek, and not after Aaron, and that Jesus is that Priest has some far-reaching consequences and implications in this epistle.

It implies first of all that the Levitical priesthood and system of worship were inadequate and due to be replaced. "If therefore perfection were by the Levitical priesthood . . . what further need was there that another priest should rise after the order of Melchizedek, and not be called after the order of Aaron?" (7:11). You can almost hear the pique in the voice of the Hebrews as they uttered these words. But the simple fact is that perfection, in the sense of the conscience being perfectly at rest as regards sin, was never attained under that priesthood, for "the law could never with those sacrifices which those priests offered year by year continually make the comers thereunto perfect. For then would they not have ceased to be offered? because that the worshippers once purged should have had no more conscience of sins. But in those sacrifices there is a remembrance again made of sins every year" (10:2,3);

71

for on the annual Day of Atonement the same national sins of the past were confessed over the head of the scape-goat (Lev. 16:21). The fact that a priest of another order was to arise did imply most certainly that the former priesthood was inadequate and the burdened soul should have welcomed the arrival of the new order with joy and relief.

More important, however, was the implication that the law and covenant under which the priesthood was set up was also declared inadequate and due to be replaced. "For the priesthood being changed, there is made of necessity a change also of the law" (7:12) and that in turn meant a "disannulling" of the foregoing commandment because of its "weakness and unprofitableness" (for the law made nothing perfect) and the bringing in of a better hope by which we draw nigh to God (7:18,19). Furthermore, in the Old Testament it had always been prophesied that one day God was going to make a new covenant with the house of Israel and with the house of Judah (Jer. 31:31-34). In that God spoke of a new covenant, what was it but that He thereby rendered the former one obsolete and that for the good reason, it says, of its "weakness and unprofitableness" and the fact that "it made nothing perfect." What is meant by those phrases we shall see in a moment. Jesus, in His capacity as our heavenly Melchizedek, is now shown to be the Surety and Mediator of a better covenant, established on better promises and conferring better benefits on its recipients. All of this means the old covenant has been replaced.

What I want to suggest at this point, and this is the whole purpose of this particular chapter in our study, is that, in spite of all this, it is altogether possible for us to be attempting to live our Christian lives under an obsolete covenant, which has already proved itself to be powerless to produce what God wants from man, and we may not be enjoying the infinitely better benefits of the new one, which in God's economy has replaced the old. Obviously, we must look closely at these two covenants in order to ascertain to what degree we are still living under the old one and to what extent we may yet need to move on to live under the new.

THE OLD COVENANT

What, then, was that old covenant? It was the covenant which God made with Israel at Mount Sinai, "when He took them by the hand to lead them out of the land of Egypt." First of all, we must be clear that the word *covenant* does not mean here what we might think — an arrangement between two parties arrived at after mutual consultation. In actual fact, in neither of these two covenants was man consulted at all as to their terms. To quote Dr. G. Campbell Morgan, "The word here denotes a disposition, or undertaking, made by one party or donor by which other parties may benefit on the conditions stated by the covenant-maker." It is really much more like what we would call a will or testament. Indeed, in chapter 9 the word is actually translated "testament"; it can be translated either way.

The first statement of the old covenant in its simplest form is found in Exodus 19:5,6, when Israel was approaching Sinai. "Now, therefore, if ye will obey my voice indeed, and keep my covenant, then ye shall be a peculiar treasure unto me above all people: for all the earth is mine: and ye shall be unto me a kingdom of priests, and an holy nation." There you have it — certain blessings and privileges promised by God conditioned on certain moral requirements being fulfilled by man. In the next chapter the moral conditions that man must fulfill are amplified in the most awesome manner possible. Recounting the great incident afterwards, Moses said, "And ye came near and stood under the mountain; the mountain burned with fire unto the midst of heaven, with darkness, clouds, and thick darkness. And the Lord spake unto you out of the midst of the fire; ye heard the voice of words, but saw no similitude [form], only ye heard a voice. And he declared unto you his covenant which he commanded you to perform, even ten commandments" (Deut. 4:11-13). Ten times they literally and audibly heard God speak, "Thou shalt . . . Thou shalt not. . . ." What an event it was! "Did ever people hear the voice of God speaking out of the midst of the fire, as thou hast heard, and live?" asked Moses afterwards (Deut. 4:33).

Then in a later chapter, God expounded further the promises He was making on His part, telling them that He would be their all-providing God, that He would give them the land of promise and would be an enemy to their enemies (Exod. 23:22-31), and all on the old condition of obedience to His law. The prospects appeared to Israel thoroughly exciting and the conditions perfectly reasonable and in their naiveté they felt themselves well able to fulfill them; and on each occasion they said, "All that the Lord has spoken to us will we do."

Then for final ratification, the covenant was written in a book and read in the audience of all the people and the blood of a sacrificial beast was sprinkled on both the book and the people, as the ritual was for making covenants in those days. That sprinkled blood signified the death of either party if he violated the covenant, rather along the line of the oft-repeated Old Testament phrase, "God do so to me and more also if. . . ." In having the book sprinkled, God was in effect saying, "May I die if I fail to keep the promises of the covenant" — an utter impossibility, of course! And in having the people sprinkled, He was in effect saying, "May you die if you fail to keep the conditions of this covenant" — an ominous probability!

There, then, are the historical facts of the making of this first covenant between God and man. Its terms were quite simple, "This do, and thou shalt live." On the other hand, the terms clearly inferred, "This fail to do, and thou shalt die." There is a long chapter toward the end of the Book of Deuteronomy (chapter 28), the first part of which enumerates with great poetic beauty the marvelous prosperity and blessing which would come upon Israel if she obeyed the law of God. The second part of the chapter, and this is by far the largest part, enumerates the curses that will come upon her if she refuses to obey. It makes terrible, even ghastly reading; it is difficult even to get oneself to finish the chapter. In any event, they did not keep it, although God sent them countless prophets, "rising up early and sending them," as the quaint phrase often reiterated in the Old Testament puts it. They never would, or could, walk truly in the ways of God, nor would they heed their prophets and return to the Lord in repentance. It was an external code of ethics which was not native to fallen man — written down on tables of stone, but not yet "on the fleshly tables of the heart." And so, ultimately, the wrath of God came upon them to the uttermost and they were carried away captive into Babylon. So it was that all they inherited from the law were the curses, and history records the accuracy of those prophecies of doom. The commandment which was ordained to life, had they obeyed it, they found to be unto death because they disobeyed.

This covenant, shorn of its Judaistic rituals, is still the covenant that the natural man understands best. The man in the street, if he thinks about his relationship with God at all, thinks of it on the basis of an exterior code of ethics which he must obey. "This do and thou shalt live" is simple and clear to him; do the best you can, do not harm anybody, fulfill your duty, and if there is a God, He will be pleased with you; and if there is a heaven, you will go there.

This is also the covenant to which the Christian brought out of Egypt naturally gravitates. "This do, and thou shalt live" is the system so often under which he seeks to run his Christian life. And, as has been mentioned in a previous chapter, it is so natural to feel that to be more deeply blessed, to find fullest peace with God, to be more greatly used by Him in His service, we must approximate more nearly the higher standards of a holy life, spend more time in prayer, be more involved in the life of the church, give our "bodies to be burned and our goods to feed the poor," and so on, and so on. How else can we expect blessing from God, if not in this way? Is not this what we have always been told from the pulpit, and even conference platforms? Of course, our thinking is not always so clearly expressed as this, but all sorts of attitudes we adopt and things we do are really subtle variants of the way of works. At first it all sounds fine and the promised blessing only just around the corner.

But what if we fail to do these things? What if we never

succeed in attaining? Then, obviously, the other side of the covenant must come into force: "This fail to do, and thou shalt die." And the fact is, we have not done it, we have not attained; we have not loved as the law of God demands that we should, none of us, not even the most consecrated, and all we have inherited from that old covenant is death — that is, reproach and condemnation. We feel that we can only make another attempt and try harder; but we shall only fail again, to be involved in an even deeper sense of guilt. What a load to carry! Little wonder that Paul talks about the law being weak and unprofitable and making nothing perfect.

THE OLD WAY OF THINKING

All the time this old way slips into our thinking and teaching. In writing these lines, I referred to a book of a great Bible teacher of a former day and my eye fell on the place where he was extolling the wonder of the fact that "the eternal God has entered into covenant with faithful and believing souls . . . the condescension of it and the honour and advantage placed within our reach by this relationship." For a moment I followed him in the wonder of it and then I stopped. But man, what if I have not been a faithful and believing soul? — and I know I have not — then I do not qualify. The honor and advantage of it are not within my reach, after all. Has God not got anything more for me than that? That sort of message (and we can all give it, for it sounds so plausible) does not do a thing for me except to set me striving to be that faithful, obedient soul and to condemn me when I fail.

All of us are preachers; we are preaching to our own hearts, if to no one else. But what sort of message do we preach? Apart from the revelation of the Holy Spirit, we all preach the wrong message to our hearts. To change the metaphor, we all naturally dial the wrong number, and on that number we always hear the voice that comes from Sinai. As a result, our Christian lives are a striving to fulfill conditions and a struggle to attain. And even if we do not do much of this (and in actual fact most of us don't), we feel we ought to and we are left with a bad conscience. That is the old covenant all over!

This, then, is what I mean by trying to live our Christian lives as under the old covenant. What is lacking? Make no mistake, there is nothing lacking with the law of God propounded from Sinai. The Ten Commandments are an eternal revelation of God's character and of His will for man and are not for one moment abrogated by the new covenant. "Do we make void the law through faith?" asks Paul; "God forbid: yea, we establish the law," as we shall also see in a moment. What is lacking is that this beautiful law, these high standards, this good advice comes to us as an exterior code of ethics. To borrow from the Exodus picture, it is something written on tables of stone — a method propounded in a book or written on a pamphlet, earnest advice given from a pulpit, and we are all the time trying to obey something exterior to ourselves. More than that, this exterior code of ethics is something that is not native to us; we are all fallen men — sinners — and it is not native to us to love God with all our hearts and our neighbors as ourselves. It is not native to us to love our enemies and bless those that curse us. The native thing is for us to hate our enemies and resent those that curse us. Being what we are, we will never make it. "The law is spiritual, but I am carnal, sold under sin" (Rom. 7:14).

It is, therefore, only too possible for the child of God, in all sincerity, to be trying to live under a covenant which cannot give life in that it is "weak through the flesh" and which in God's economy has been rendered obsolete by the new and better one that we shall see Jesus has brought in.

> Under the law with its ten-fold lash,
>   Learning, alas, how true,
> That the more I tried, the sooner I died,
>   While the law cried, You! You! You!
>
> Hopelessly still did the battle rage,
>   O, wretched man, my cry,
> And deliverance I sought, by some penance bought,
>   While my heart cried, I! I! I!
>
> Then came a day when my struggling ceased,
>   And trembling in every limb,
> At the foot of the tree, where One died for me,
>   My heart cried, Him! Him! Him!

The New Covenant

So now we come to the new covenant of which Jesus, our heavenly High Priest, is both Surety and Mediator. It was prophesied long before in the Old Testament, even in the days when the old covenant was still in force. It was as if God sighed and said, "If My purposes for Israel and the world are to come to pass, they will never be realized this way; they will only come to pass as a result of an entirely new covenant on an entirely new basis."

This covenant, like the first, is not arrived at by mutual agreement, but is a disposition, or testament, whereby certain benefits are conferred on other parties on conditions stated by the covenant-maker — only this time we do not seem able to find what the conditions are, and that for the simple reason that there are none. No conditions at all — save the obviously implied one, that the beneficiary confesses his total lack of the blessings promised and his desperate need of them. In other words, it is a covenant of grace whereby God loves us as we are and does not require worthiness or attainments from us before He blesses us, because He knows we cannot produce them. It is a blessed one-sided covenant of love without strings and the responsibility for the implementation of the terms is put in the hands of a Mediator, the Lord Jesus, who is going to be faithful to Him who has appointed Him to act for us.

As we cast a first look over the terms of the covenant, we make the surprising discovery that what were necessary conditions for us to fulfill under the old covenant are the very blessings promised under the new. The great condition for the realization of blessing under the old covenant was "if you will obey my voice." But under the new that is the very blessing promised, "you *shall* obey my voice," and Jesus is to be the Surety or Guarantor that that will be implemented in us and by us. Under the old covenant, obedience was demanded; under the new, it is secured. What a new world is this! In the school of grace, the bottom is at the top and the back is in the front. We shall have to be ready for all sorts of surprises as we explore further this exciting new covenant of grace.

We come now to the first and major benefit promised. "This is the covenant that I will make with the house of Israel; after those days, saith the Lord, I will put my laws into their mind and write them in their hearts" (Jer. 31:33). The law of God is no longer to be an exterior code of ethics to which we pledge obedience, but it is going to be something put within us, written in the heart and put into the mind, made a part of a person, so it is not merely something he feels he *ought* to do, but what he *wants* to. In other words, holiness and love are going to be principles that are native to us. We can hardly believe it, we can hardly see the first glimmer of such a "nativeness" in ourselves, but if it is grace that is going to do the work, then we do not need to present to God anything but our emptiness in the matter — it is our one qualification.

It is not only in the quotation from Jeremiah 31 that we have this extraordinary grace promised, but in other Old Testament prophecies too, notably that in Ezekiel 36: "A new heart also will I give you, and a new spirit will I put within you, and I will take away the stony heart out of your flesh, and I will give you an heart of flesh. I will put my spirit within you and *cause* you to walk in my statutes, and ye *shall* keep my judgments, and do them" (Ezek. 36:26,27). How about that — "I will *cause* you to walk in my statutes"! And all that because "I will put my spirit within you." Amid all the sorrows of the broken law and the necessary disciplines it involved, the prophets saw a yet more glorious day for Israel, at the center of which would be this new covenant, mediated by Jesus.

What was prophecy in the Old Testament is realization in the New. Paul says to the Corinthians that they were "the epistle of Christ, ministered by us, written not with ink, but with the Spirit of the living God, not in tables of stone, but in fleshy tables of the heart" (2 Cor. 3:3). To the Philippians he writes, "It is God that worketh in you both to will and to do of His good pleasure" (Phil. 2:13). And in the last chapter of the Epistle to the Hebrews he expresses the prayer that God may make his readers perfect (fully equipped) to do His will, "working in you that which is pleasing in His sight." Note this repeated phrase about the in-working of God in the heart of a believer. In other words, *grace puts into us what God wants out of us.* If God wants holiness, love for others, gentleness, sacrificial service out of me, He will have to put them all into me, because they are just not there naturally — but this is just what is promised. If sometimes you come to a place where God is asking out of you what is not in you, just confess that fact to Him and do so in confidence that He is pledged to work it in you.

When the world sees this happening in the lives of Christians, they just cannot understand it. They see the life of a new Christian take another turn. He becomes absorbed in the worship and service of the Lord. All day Sunday finds him at church with his new-found friends. During the week he is out for a prayer meeting or a Bible study. He is also taking his part in outreach activities to bring the gospel to others. Many of the old worldly pleasures and interests that used to absorb him seem to be cut out and his old friends are quite mystified. Sometimes the world sees splendid, highly qualified young people casting aside the prospect of successful careers to go to backward parts of the world as missionaries, or making extravagant sacrifices for Christ in other ways. The world cannot understand them (sometimes their own parents can't) and I think there is one question it wants to ask of any such Christian:

"Do you *have* to do these things?"

The answer the Christian would give is, "No, I don't *have* to at all."

"Then why in the world are you doing them?"

"Because I *want* to!"

"You really want to do these things? I am amazed!"

To do these things would, to the man of the world, be hard labor indeed. The Christian, however, would doubtless hasten to add, "It has not always been like this with me. There was a time when I did not love the things of God, when, if I thought of them at all, it was only as things I *ought* to do. But there came a day when I met Jesus and there has been a big change on the inside, and now I *want* to!"

Do you see what has happened? God has been writing His

law in his heart; grace has been putting into him what God wants out of him. Sometimes God works the willingness, desire, and capability into a person, even before, maybe a long time before, He calls for it out of him. That is a hardship indeed for him; he is "champing at the bit," longing to serve, only complaining that he does not seem to have the opportunity to spend and be spent. When at last the call does come, he is ready to go and no hardship stops him. Only so can the words of Jesus be seen to be true, "My yoke is easy and my burden is light."

The Holy Spirit is the One by whom this godly in-working in our hearts is carried on. He was the great Gift that the ascended Lord Jesus received of the Father for His waiting church. When each sinner comes in penitence to put faith in Christ crucified, he is sealed with that Holy Spirit of promise, who comes to live in him and proceeds with the work of progressively writing God's law on his heart. By His presence within us, Jesus lives again His life through us. In this way there is the fulfillment of Ezekiel's prophecy, "I will put my spirit within them and cause them to walk in my statutes." In this way, as we have said, the condition of obedience to be fulfilled under the old covenant is the proffered blessing under the new.

Even the Ten Commandments, with their reiterated "thou shalts" and "thou shalt nots" can be regarded as promises under the new covenant. Oh, for such a faith in grace that will see them as such and will present them to God for His fulfillment!

It can be seen, then, that the new covenant is in no sense an abrogation of the law of God. It is simply another way of achieving the same end — the fulfilling of the righteousness of the law. Under the first covenant it was to be the work of man, and that on pain of death, and the result was nothing but failure; under the new it is to be the work of grace, and Jesus does not fail.

Can we not see that in living under the old covenant we have really been trying to do His work for Him and falling under condemnation by our failure to do it? How greatly we need to know how to go on from living under that old covenant to living under the new.

THE NEW COVENANT IMPLEMENTED

We must now ask ourselves the question, What is the process in practical terms by which the law is thus written on our hearts?

To answer this, we must pass quickly over the next two terms of the covenant, with but a paragraph on each, and go on to the fourth. The second says, "I will be to them a God and they shall be to me a people." As a result of their departure from Him, God had had to say to them, as He has to say to us sometimes, "Not my people" (Hos. 1:9), and we have the sad sight of God left without a people and of a people left without a God. But under grace, that broken relationship can be restored and that just as often as it gets broken, so that it can be said of us, "In the place where it was said unto them, Ye are not my people, there it shall be said unto them, Ye are the sons of the living God" (Hos. 1:10). I like the word "in the place"; in the place of failure, in the place where God had to chasten us, there grace will reach us, if we will humble ourselves to acknowledge our sin.

Then follows the third promise: "And they shall not teach every man his neighbour, and every man his brother, saying, Know the Lord; for all shall know me, from the least to the greatest" (Heb. 8:11). Although the saint cannot hear too much of Jesus and loves to hear the Word of God opened to him, there is a teaching he does not need. It is the teaching that professes to tell him *how* — how to know Jesus, how to work for God, how to read his Bible, how to win souls. Some people love to tell us how. All we lack in the Christian life, it seems, is know-how. The saint does not need that teaching. He already knows the Lord; he is already having first-hand insights and experiences of the grace of God and, knowing the Lord, he knows everything else. And all this is "from the least to the greatest." What a picture of a true fellowship meeting, all on the same level, from the newest Christian to the most experienced leader, from the one with little education to the most high-born — all sharing their insights and experience of Jesus. How out of place in such a situation it would be for someone to start to give know-how teaching! I tried to do that myself on one occasion in a fellowship meeting in East Africa and I was gently told by an African brother afterwards that it did not quite fit.

Now we come to the important fourth promise of the covenant. It begins with the little word *for*, which tells us the reason for all that has gone before, or, if you will, the process by which all know the Lord, by which those who were not His people become His people again and especially by which He writes His law on our hearts. "For I will be merciful to their unrighteousness and their sins and iniquities I will remember no more."

That "for" gives us the clue to the other promises of the covenant. The only way to know the Lord is to know Him as a forgiving God and that means our taking the position of a sinner who needs His forgiveness, and doing so, if necessary, many times. We do not get to know Him merely by studying our Bibles, important as that is, but by going to the foot of His cross where love and mercy find us again. What a God!

Then the only way in which we enter again into that relationship where we know Him as our God and ourselves as His people is by experiencing Him as a forgiving God. Because He is the One who delights in mercy, we need not suffer broken fellowship with Him for any longer than it takes us to repent.

Above all, it is by many experiences of His forgiveness that He writes His law on my heart. He deals with me first on this matter and then on another and wrestles with me until I confess again that He is right and I am wrong; and immediately I find Him putting His arm around me and being merciful to my unrighteousness and assuring me that my sin and iniquity He now remembers no more. That would be blessing enough, but in the process He writes the opposite of what I am confessing on my heart. And so I go on, repenting and being forgiven, first over one thing and then over another, and as I walk this way, He works a progressive holiness in me. I find I do not get love for a difficult brother by asking for love, but rather by repenting of the unlove in my heart (God says, "Call it hatred!") and being forgiven that sin. This sometimes involves me in putting things right with the other. And then I find without much asking that Jesus gives me His love for him and my relationship with him changes, sometimes very dramatically. I find I do not get faith by asking for faith, but by confessing unbelief and calling it sin and being forgiven; and then automatically faith and confidence in the Lord takes its place and I am at peace. And so on, for every other quality I find I lack. A desperate asking for this or that needed quality can be only a form of struggling. But a deep confessing that I am empty of that quality — and that because of my sin — makes me a fit candidate for the grace of God and He does not fail to meet me.

This will involve us in submitting to many convictions of sin from the Holy Spirit and having to say yes to humbling revelations of the wrong ways self acts and reacts. But it will also mean many sweet experiences of mercy and forgiveness at the feet of Jesus. But this is the way in which God's law gets written on our hearts and we are made progressively partakers of the mind and disposition of the Lord Jesus. It is not that our old nature is improved, but His is imparted. You see, potentially He has been in us ever since we first received Him, but we have not been able to share His life and nature because of our lack of self-judgment with regard to the ways of our old nature.

The man involved in this process is largely unaware of any progressive holiness in himself; he is only conscious of new points on which he has to come to Jesus as a sinner and receive forgiveness and cleansing. But others see and feel the difference and are so grateful for the new sweetness and grace about him. It is just another case of what Oswald Chambers called "conscious repentance leading to unconscious holiness." I prefer it that way, don't you? I don't think a man who is consciously holy is very attractive. In the nature of the case, holiness and victory are largely unconscious, because one is often unaware that certain things do not arouse him, as they once did. He is walking in peace with Jesus and he is conscious only when there is a failure in holiness; and as he judges himself there, Jesus to that degree expands further His territory in him.

Now this covenant has not only a mediator, but a surety. A mediator is one who negotiates the covenant and administrates its provisions, but a surety is something different. He is the guarantor that the covenant will be fulfilled and if there is any failure on the part of either party, he is responsible. Solomon, in the Book of Proverbs, said, "He that is surety for a stranger shall smart for it." A surety is sometimes involved in paying out large sums of money on behalf of the one for whom he has stood surety. As our heavenly High Priest, Jesus is not only the Mediator of this new covenant, but its Surety. He has become personally involved in it and is personally responsible for any failure in its performance. There is no chance, of course, that He will have to make good any failure on God's part, but what about the failure on ours? Whereas it is true that it is a one-sided covenant, sin is still sin and God is still holy and our hearts will often say, "How can God go on with a sinner like me?" Thank God, there is a Surety and He is in heaven making intercession for us. Jesus and His one offering are the guarantee that God is not going to allow even our sins to thwart His purposes for us, or disannul His covenant. They were all anticipated and settled by Jesus to God's satisfaction in His body on the tree, even before one of them was committed and it needs only recourse to our Surety in repentance again, and the work of grace goes on apace. What a comfort to have a Surety who guarantees it all!

May I share with you how I first saw the truth that grace puts into us what God wants out of us and the liberty it brought to my heart? As a young Christian I once saw a man walking the streets carrying sandwich boards on his back and front and over his head, on which were inscribed texts of Scripture — you know, encouraging ones, like "The wicked shall be turned into hell!"

I said to myself, *I think people like that do more harm than good.*

A little voice whispered in my heart, *But would you do the same for Me?*

Yes, I suppose so, I said, *if You really wanted me to!*

All right, then, get boards and carry texts around the streets!

I was aghast! I couldn't; I wouldn't.

Then don't expect any more blessing from Me until you do so.

I lost all the joy of the Lord and I was in darkness for, I cannot remember how long. I was in utter misery — no more blessing from God, I felt, until I did this, to me, excruciatingly difficult thing!

At last the Lord met me in my misery. I cannot remember what it was He used, but I came to the point where I said to myself, *I am miserable, but who is making me miserable? Does God make His children miserable? Of course not; then who is making me miserable?* It came to me it could only be Satan and it dawned on me that that little voice I heard was not the voice of God, but Satan simulating God's voice. Jesus had said that the devil was a liar. In that moment I was free from my bondage and rejoicing in the Lord again. I said, "Lord, I think I have learned something today; and I think I'll recognize that voice of Satan when he comes challenging me to do things You have not put in me; and on principle, I'm not going to do them. I hope I will not make a mistake, Lord, and excuse myself from doing things You are obviously wanting me to do. But surely I *can* trust You to put into me what You want out of me, so that I have the inner desire and a joy in doing it."

The interesting thing is that God did just that in almost the same sort of matter. Years later, I was part of a team of students conducting an evangelistic mission in a working-class parish. We wanted to do something that would stir the district and make them know that something was on. We hit on the idea of obtaining a truck and putting on it a huge poster: War Declared on Public Enemy No. 1 — That Old Serpent, the Devil. Then, as a team of young people, we climbed onto the truck and went around the parish singing gospel choruses and announcing the meetings, with gladness in our hearts and joy on our faces. No painful legalistic conpulsion here; we wanted to do it and we were doing so with Jesus. And I am sure the Lord used the joyful testimony of it to some hearts.

Let us go on, then, from living under the old covenant, with all its bondage and guilt, to living with Jesus under the new.

Let Us Go On

From Living in the Holy Place
to Living in the
Holiest of All

Then verily the first covenant had also ordinances of divine service, and a worldly sanctuary. For there was a tabernacle made; the first, wherein was the candlestick, and the table, and the shewbread; which is called the sanctuary [Holy Place]. And after the second veil, the tabernacle which is called the Holiest of all; which had the golden censer, and the ark of the covenant, overlaid round about with gold, wherein was the golden pot that had manna, and Aaron's rod that budded, and the tables of the covenant; and over it the cherubims of glory shadowing the mercy seat; of which we cannot now speak particularly.

Now when these things were thus ordained, the priest went always into the first tabernacle, accomplishing the service of God. But into the second went the high priest alone once every year, not without blood, which he offered for himself, and for the errors of the people:
    the Holy Spirit this signifying that the way into the Holiest of all was not yet made manifest, while as the first tabernacle was yet standing; which was a figure for the time then present, in which were offered both gifts and sacrifices, that could not make him that did the service perfect, as pertaining to the conscience; which stood only in meats and drinks, and divers washings, and carnal ordinances, imposed on them until the time of reformation.

But Christ being come an high priest of good things to come, by a greater and more perfect tabernacle, not made with hands, that is to say, not of this building; neither by the blood of goats and calves,
    but by his own blood he entered in once into the Holy Place, having obtained eternal redemption for us.

For if the blood of bulls and goats, and the ashes of an heifer sprinkling the unclean, sanctifieth to the purifying of the flesh:
    how much more shall the blood of Christ, who through the eternal Spirit offered himself without spot to God, purge your conscience from dead works to serve the living God?

    Having, therefore, brethren, boldness to enter into the Holiest by the blood of Jesus, by a new and living way, which he hat consecrated for us, through the veil, that is to say, his flesh . . . Let us draw near. . . .

                                        —Hebrews 9:1-14; 10:19-22

5

Let Us Go On

From Living in the Holy Place
to Living in the
Holiest of All

WE COME NOW to the culminating point of the whole epistle, a passage of just four verses (10:19-22) beginning with the words, "Having therefore, brethren, boldness to enter the Holiest by the blood of Jesus . . . let us draw near. . . ."

The apostle Paul has already brought before us successively the promised land, the high priest, and the covenant under which he operated. Now he introduces us to the actual sanctuary in which he served. The sanctuary in which the high priest ministered was, of course, the tabernacle that Israel carried with them on their journeys through the wilderness. This tabernacle was divided into two compartments, the Holy Place and the Holiest of All, or as it is sometimes called, the Holy of Holies. These two compartments speak to us of two degrees of proximity to God in which the believer may dwell. One is pictured by the Holy Place, the other by the Holiest of All, and the call of this epistle is that we should go on from living in the first to living in the second.

These particular verses are the peak of the entire epistle toward which Paul has been working and from which the rest of the epistle flows. They begin with the words "Having therefore. . . ." Someone has said that when we come across the word *therefore* in Scripture we should always ask ourselves what it is "there for." Obviously, Paul is referring to all he has said earlier about our heavenly High Priest, the new covenant which He mediates and the sufficiency of His once-for-all offering for sin. Building on all that, he now urges us to enter the Holiest of All. For the same reason, I would make bold to suggest that this particular part of our study is perhaps more important for the reader than any other.

Let us look together at this tabernacle and its two partitions. When today we gaze at the huge and handsome church which Spurgeon built to house his overflowing congregation in London and hear it called "The Metropolitan Tabernacle," we get the idea that the word *tabernacle* must always signify something rather grandiose. The very opposite is the case in the Bible, where the word simply means a tent, a temporary movable dwelling in contrast to a permanent one which has foundations. The tabernacle in the wilderness was just that, a portable place of worship, of no great proportions, which could be dismantled and erected again, as the Israelites moved from place to place in the desert. The pattern of this tabernacle was not left to man's devising. Every detail of it was given to Moses by God during the weeks he was alone in Mount Sinai and all parts of its structure and furniture were to have a deep significance. Indeed, they are said to be "the patterns of things in the heavens," a visual representation of spiritual and heavenly realities.

There was, first of all, an outer court curtained off from the rest of the camp, but open to the skies. Here one encountered the brazen altar, where the daily burnt offerings and other sacrifices were offered, and then a laver of brass, where the priests would wash themselves before entering the tabernacle proper in the middle of the outer court. This tabernacle was not open to the skies but was covered with badger skins. It was simply a tent, not very different on the outside from those in which the Israelites lived. Theirs were covered with badger skins; so was Jehovah's. And that is what the tabernacle was, above all else — not so much a place of worship, but the dwelling place of God on earth; only secondarily was it a place where they worshiped Him. And the surprising thing is that that dwelling place was so similar to those of the Israelites which surrounded it; but it was deliberately so planned, as we shall see in a moment.

In contrast to its exterior, the interior of the tabernacle was glorious indeed, abounding in gold and hangings in gorgeous colors. In the first compartment, the Holy Place, stood the golden candlestick, the table of shewbread, and the altar of incense.[1] Here only the priests, the sons of Aaron, were allowed to go, and they did so every day, accomplishing the service of God.

Farther in and beyond it was the Holiest of All; it was this part that symbolized the very dwelling place of God. It housed just one thing: the ark of the covenant, the chief contents of which were the two tables of the covenant. The golden lid of the ark was called the mercy seat, with two cherubim of glory fashioned out of it, and overshadowing it with their wings. The Holiest of All was always full of brilliant light, although there was no window; an unearthly luminosity emanated from between the cherubim. This was a sign of God's manifested presence, what the old rabbinical commentators called the *Shekinah*. It was presumably the base of the pillar of cloud and fire which always rested over the tabernacle and doubtless it partook of the same characteristics — fire with a sheath of cloud which modulated its heat but enabled its light to shine when there was no natural light. So there was a progression with

---

[1]Although Hebrews 9 puts the golden altar of incense in the Holiest of All, it is clear from Exodus 30 that it was actually situated in the Holy Place, where the high priest burnt sweet incense on it every morning. One can only assume that the reason why Hebrews 9 speaks of it as being in the Holiest of All is that, although incense was offered on it every morning, by far and away its most important function was within the veil, when on the Day of Atonement once a year the high priest went in there. He took with him a censer full of burning coals of fire and incense from off the golden altar, the purpose being "that the cloud of incense might cover the mercy seat that is upon the testimony that he die not." Its further association with the Holiest of All is seen by the fact that it was the nearest piece of furniture to it, being placed exactly opposite the mercy seat, but on the other side of the veil.

regard to the illumination of the whole tabernacle; the outer court was lit by the sun, the Holy Place by the golden candlesticks, but the Holiest of All by the *Shekinah* glory. This was the awesome sign that God was at home. Little wonder that Aaron was warned by God not to come any time he chose into the Holiest lest he die, "for I will appear in the cloud upon the mercy seat" (Lev. 16:2). It was the holiest place on earth for Israel and it was death for any man to enter there, except for the high priest, and he only once a year. The priests, the sons of Aaron, could enter the Holy Place at any time, but the Holiest of All, never. Only the high priest could do so on the great Day of Atonement, and then not without the blood of a sin offering, which he sprinkled on the mercy seat and before the mercy seat.

Dividing the Holy Place from the Holiest of All, there hung a heavy curtain, known as the veil. In itself it was of great beauty, "of blue and purple and scarlet and fine twined linen of cunning work," as the text has it, and embroidered into it were the figures of the cherubim. Its main purpose, however, was to hide the glories of the Holiest of All from the eye of sinful man, "lest he die." The fact that the high priest was allowed to lift that veil once a year was an indication that a day would ultimately come when man would not always be excluded from the vision of God. But till then, that veil remained.

". . . That I May Dwell Among Them"

Now what is the meaning of this tabernacle? In one place it is called "the tabernacle of witness," but what did it witness to? It testified to God's age-long desire to dwell among men. He was not content to have created man; from the very beginning He desired to dwell with him and have fellowship with him. That this was the witness of the tabernacle is seen by the fact that when God first gave instructions for the gathering of the materials for its construction, He said, "And let them make me a sanctuary that I may dwell among them." As we have suggested, it was something more than a place of worship or church, as we know it today; it was God's very sanctuary, where He could dwell among them and where the awesome

Shekinah cloud of glory, symbol of His presence, might rest.

I imagine when God's intention thus to dwell among them was made known, it did not please them very much. Indeed, it might have terrified them, for it was generally understood among them that "no man can see God and live." Indeed, when one of the patriarchs or a prophet had a vision of God and found himself still alive, no one was more surprised than himself. Said Jacob, "I have seen God face to face and my life is preserved." To have seen Him and yet to be alive to tell the tale was considered a special mark of His favor and of His intentions for good. And here was the proposition of having Him live right in the midst of their tents all day and every day, right next door, so to speak! This was bringing Him a little too close for comfort! They might well have uttered the words Isaiah used later, "Who among us shall dwell with the everlasting burnings?"

Had they expressed themselves in this way, God would doubtless have made it known that there was no need to fear His coming to dwell among them, and that for two reasons. First, He was going to dwell in a tent. They dwelt in tents and He was going to dwell in one too; and the badger skins of His tent would hide the brightness of His glory so that they should not die. There was also to be that veil within it, screening the Holiest of All from the Holy Place, which would hide the most intense expression of His glory, so that the priests going about their duties in the Holy Place could do so without danger.

Secondly, right at the heart of everything, behind the veil, there was the mercy seat upon which was sprinkled atoning blood, showing unmistakeably that God's purpose in dwelling among them was only to bring them His mercy for their misery and His grace for their guilt.

That was something of what the tabernacle witnessed to in those days. It was more, however; it was a foreshadowing of "good things to come" as this epistle puts it, which good things are now fulfilled in Jesus Christ. And we in the Christian era are bidden to see it as such and gain fuller insights into Him by means of it. The whole tabernacle is to be taken by us as a picture of the Lord Jesus, for He is the One by whom God has come to dwell among men in reality. The very name by which

He was called when He came as a babe to Bethlehem denotes this: "And they shall call his name Emmanuel, which being interpreted is, God with us." Then again John 1:14 says, "The Word was made flesh and dwelt among us." God's great desire to dwell among men was at last fulfilled in Him, not in symbol but in fact, although it will not be fully culminated until He returns to establish the kingdom of God on earth. Then in very deed and universally it will be true — "the tabernacle of God is with men and he will dwell with them and they shall be his people, and God himself shall be with them, and be their God" (Rev. 21:3).

Moreover, the way in which God has come to dwell among men in His Son is exactly as foreshadowed by the tabernacle of old. It is significant that in the verse I have just quoted, "the Word was made flesh and dwelt among us," the word *dwelt* is literally in the Greek *tabernacled*. This means that the flesh of the Lord Jesus was the tent in which Deity lived while here on earth. We live in tents of flesh and blood; the Deity willed to live in one too, just to be near us. And the badger skins of that tent would hide His full glory from the eyes of mortal men lest they be overwhelmed at the sight. As Charles Wesley's Christmas hymn puts it,

> Veiled in flesh the Godhead see.
> Hail the incarnate Deity!

The humanity of the Lord Jesus, though giving expression to the character of the One within, was intended, then, to hide rather than reveal. Though it is true that He said, "He that hath seen me hath seen the Father," that can only refer to the character of the Father. The glory of the Deity was hidden by His flesh out of consideration for man. How else could the twelve disciples have companied with Deity as they did?

This is made more abundantly clear when we consider the veil that separates the Holiest of All from the Holy Place. Hebrews 10:20 tells us what that veil symbolizes: "the veil, that is to say, his flesh." It was a beautiful veil, good to look at doubtless, but its main purpose was to hide the glory within. So it is that when Jesus came as a babe to Bethlehem, lived as a boy in Nazareth, and walked as a man through Galilee, Judea, and Jerusalem, all that men could see was the veil — beautiful indeed, but still a veil. Horatio Bonar says, "The miracles of grace wrought during His ministry were like the waving of the folds of that veil before men's eyes, letting some of the rays of the inner majesty through. So were His words of grace from day to day." On one occasion God quite deliberately lifted a corner of that veil when Jesus was on the mountain with three of His disciples, "and Jesus was transfigured before them and His face did shine as the sun and His raiment was white as the light." But they could not bear the sight and "they were sore afraid." And so the veil was quickly dropped again and they were commanded to tell the vision to no man till He was risen from the dead.

The greatest cause for comfort, however, is the fact that Jesus has come to dwell among us as our blood-sprinkled Mercy Seat. Romans 3:25 says of Jesus: "Whom God hath set forth to be a propitiation through faith in his blood," and interestingly, in the Greek the word *propitiation* in this place is exactly the same as "mercy seat," and means "a place of propitiation." Jesus is not only the tabernacle to us, but more important, our mercy seat within that tabernacle. When we remind ourselves that under the mercy seat within the ark lie the two tables of the law which we have so often broken, we wonder how that seat can be anything more to us than one of judgment — until we see the blood stains on it. It is simply the blood of Jesus, shed on the cross and sprinkled now before God that makes Jesus a mercy seat, a place of propitiation, to us rather than a judgment seat. Do not be afraid of this word *propitiation* or substitute a word like *expiation* for it, as the Revised Standard Version does. "Propitiation" presupposes the anger of God against sin, and it could be that some of the revisers backed off from that conception and chose this other word. But the fact is that the just anger of God needed to be propitiated with regard to human sin and the blood of Jesus Christ has gloriously and fully done just that. That work of propitiation is utterly sufficient for every last sin of which men are capable and it means that the God who dwells among us in Christ does so not to condemn us but to bring us, to repeat the phrase, His mercy for our miseries and His grace for our guilt.

THE HOLY PLACE AND THE HOLIEST OF ALL

If the whole tabernacle is to be seen as a type of the Lord Jesus, what are we to make of the two compartments within that tabernacle, the Holy Place and the Holiest of All? Their significance is first historical and then experiential. As to the historical significance, we are left in no doubt by the epistle, because the apostle says quite clearly that the Holy Place was "a figure of the time then present" (9:9), which phrase signifies the whole Old Testament era, when "gifts and sacrifices that could not make him that did the service perfect as pertaining to the conscience" were still being offered and when the "way into the Holiest was not yet made manifest." This era also extended to the period covered by the four Gospels in the New Testament, because, although Jesus had come in the flesh, that very flesh was itself the veil, hiding the full glory of God. Those who knew Christ then "knew him [only] after the flesh" (a phrase Paul uses elsewhere), and that was as true of the disciples as of anyone else. Even in the time of the Gospels men could get only so far in their relationship with God and no further.

If the Holy Place represents the time then present, the Holiest of All represents the time now present, the great feature of which is that the veil, that is to say, His flesh, has been rent and the way into the Holiest made manifest for all to enter. As Jesus expired on the cross outside the city, a great symbolic act took place within the city: "And, behold, the veil of the temple was rent in twain from the top to the bottom." The age-long separation between God and man was at last removed through His offering up of Himself on the cross for us. Not only so, but Jesus, rising again from the dead and ascending into heaven, entered as our great High Priest into the Holiest by His own blood, "having obtained eternal redemption for us," leaving the door, so to speak, open for us too. Indeed, we are specifically told in Hebrews 6:20 that He entered in as the forerunner, and where the forerunner goes others follow. When the everlasting doors lifted up their heads and welcomed the King of Glory back, it was known that He was entering only as the forerunner of a great company of others, mighty sinners saved by mightier grace, who would enter by the same way, by His blood. A new and living way into the Holiest was opened through the veil of His flesh, consecrated for people no better than we are.

All this means that in this glorious gospel day we may know Christ no longer after the flesh (2 Cor. 5:17). We see beyond the historical Jesus, a form He took only temporarily, to know Him in spiritual reality as He really is. Pictures of the earthly Jesus in books or stained glass windows are of no help to us. We no longer look back to those who knew Him in His earthly days and say in the words of the children's hymn, "I wish I had been with them then." We know Him, and God in Him, in a way none ever knew Him then. Those days, even at their highest, pertained only to the period before the veil was rent. Something infinitely better is open to us now. We may know Him in the same way as we will know Him in heaven. Indeed, when we get there, I believe we shall find the place strangely familiar — at least, in the basic matter of how we know Him. We have already come to know Him without a veil in the Holiest while on earth and that is how we will know Him in heaven — in a heightened degree, of course, and with all impediments removed, but basically the same Lord Jesus, known in the same way. How thrilling!

These two compartments not only represent two periods in history, but two degrees of proximity to God in which the Christian can live in experience. The veil of which we have spoken was not the only veil; there was one actually at the entrance of the Holy Place itself and divided it from the outer court. But the one we are thinking of was beyond the Holy Place and divided it from the Holiest. This one did not divide between the secular and the sacred, but between the sacred and the most sacred. What we have here is not the division between the lost and the saved, nor even between the unconsecrated Christian and the consecrated, but between two degrees of proximity to God in which the Christian can live.

When in the outer court we have come first of all to the brazen
altar — a picture of Calvary's Cross — and known our sin
atoned for, and have gone on to the laver of brass — a picture of
regeneration ("the laver of regeneration" Titus 3:5 RV mg.) —
and experienced the new birth, we then have to choose where
we are going to live out our Christian lives, in the Holy Place or
the Holiest of All. If that be so, it behooves us to inquire what
the two degrees of Christian experience are, wherein they
differ, and how we may go on from the one to the other.

LIVING IN THE HOLY PLACE

First, then, what is life in the Holy Place? In those far-off
days it was a place symbolically much nearer to God than the
outer court. Nevertheless, it was only the Holy Place; there
was always the veil excluding the priests from the nearest
place. Even so with us, the Holy-Place degree of experience is
a place nearer to God and infinitely better than when we were
still in our sins, in the outer court and beyond. It is still
nonetheless only the Holy Place, a picture of the shadow
Christian life. Although historically the veil has been rent,
something very much like it still seems to be there in our
experience, excluding us from that more intimate fellowship
with God. We had hoped that we would have found in our
Christian lives a much nearer place to God and a more real
experience of His presence. Such an experience may have
eluded us for so long that we are in danger of "settling for" the
Holy Place, assuming that that is all there is in the Christian
life. In that case, we might have to admit that the Christian life
is hardly worth the enormous price that Jesus paid for it. I
remember hearing a man in an American church give his
testimony that he had felt just that. He said that as he saw
people go forward in their church service to accept Christ,
he felt almost embarrassed, fearing they would find no more
in the Christian life than he had. This is the shadow Christian life.

The Holy Place was nonetheless a place full of busy service
for God, for the priests were coming and going continually.
"Now when these things were thus ordained, the priests went

always into the first tabernacle accomplishing the service of God" (9:6). There was the golden candlestick to be replenished with oil, the shewbread to be changed, the incense to be offered, and various sacrifices to be made and even eaten there. But although all this was done in the service of God, the veil always hung between them and Him, and their acts of service must have therefore lacked the luster of reality. For us too, the Holy-Place level of experience is often a place of busy service for God too. We can be busy in many Christian activities — but only in the Holy Place with a seeming veil between us and God. When that is so, these activities are without spiritual vitality and are not lighted by His realized presence. Though trying to preach to others, we are not moved and melted by what we are teaching. The words in the King James Version "accomplishing the service of God" are translated in the Revised Standard Version, "performing their ritual duties." That is it, our acts of service have become just a string of "ritual duties"! They are only shadows of the real thing and "not the very image of the things." Not that active service is necessarily wrong; obviously, some are called of God to a life of great activity in His work. But the seeming veil between us and God deprives everything of meaningful reality.

Then we read that in the Holy Place the gifts and sacrifices offered there "could not make him that did the service perfect as pertaining to the conscience" (9:9). In spite of all they did, the priests never achieved by those means the sense of being cleared of guilt and blame in their relationship to God. We, too, find that our sacrifices and service do nothing to deal with our conscience, which is that part of us that gives us most trouble. We are struggling all along with an uneasy conscience, dogged with a sense of not being good enough and of being accused, sometimes about specific things in our lives, but more often not as acute as that — just a general and diffuse sense of not being right. And nothing we do, no service we offer, seems to be able to take it away. Reading our Bibles, spending more time in prayer, getting more involved in Christian service, and much else fail to make "him that does the service perfect as pertaining to the conscience." But we struggle on with these things in the hope that one day the skies will become blue over our heads; but they never do that way. What a pathetic sight we must be to heavenly intelligences (and such there are) as they see us performing our ritual duties, "ministering and offering oftentimes the same sacrifices that can never take away sins" (10:11). The fact is that the Christian's service is never any answer to the Christian's sin, and sin is his real problem. If the skies are to be blue for him again, it will have to be by some other way than this.

I remember one of the first times I realized I was living only in the Holy Place. I had been engaged in full-time evangelistic work in Great Britain for a number of years and I was responsible for leading an Easter conference. I had invited as speakers a team of missionaries who had come home to share with us in England what they had been learning in a deep and continuing movement of revival in East Africa. I was to take the first session each morning, while the rest of the day was to be in their hands. I had completed my message one morning and as I turned to speak with them (they had been sitting on the platform behind me), I found them all deeply moved and with tears in their eyes. They had been touched by what they had seen of Jesus in my message. But I who had given the message had not been moved at all, nor were there any tears in my eyes. That fact was enough to show me that these men had something that I did not have and I began to realize then how mechanical and even professional my service had become. I was only in the Holy Place and my cold heart was not seeing the glorious and moving reality of the very things I was speaking about. I had the shadow rather than the substance.

LIVING IN THE HOLIEST OF ALL

What, then, is life in the Holiest? It is first of all living in the light as He is in the light. When the high priest went into the Holy of Holies once a year, he found himself standing in the brightest light known on earth. It was the Shekinah glory shining out from between the cherubim over the mercy seat. In that light his own white robe showed up grey and soiled. Indeed, the purpose of his offering incense as he went in was that its cloud might cover the mercy seat and presumably give him some protection from the brightness of that light. Just so is the Holiest to us in experience. John in his first epistle tells us that the message he has to declare is that "God is light and in Him is no darkness at all" and we on our part are called to "walk in the light, as He is in the light."

In the New Testament and especially in John's writings, light and darkness are not just vague synonyms for good and evil. Light is that which reveals, darkness is that which hides. "Whatsoever doth make manifest is light" (Eph. 5:13). When a room is in darkness, we may bump into a chair and think it is the table, but when the light is turned on, the chair is seen to be the chair and the table, the table. In the same way when John says, "God is light," he means that God is the all-revealing One and His light is all the time shining on our hearts, showing up everything as it really is in His sight. He goes on to say, "And in him is no darkness at all," meaning that He cannot condone one bit of hiding or duplicity in us. But hiding is native to us all.

To live, then, in the Holiest is to consent to walk in the light as He is in the light, saying yes to whatever His light reveals without hiding or prevarication, even when to say yes means to confess ourselves to be wrong where before we thought we were right. And to admit ourselves to be wrong is invariably a real death to die. This is not very different from what Acts 9:31 calls "walking in the fear of the Lord," which is simply a conscientious willingness to say, "O God, You are right and I am wrong," whenever He shows that to be so.

This all-revealing light may not always come to us direct from God, as for instance, when reading or hearing the Word of God or praying, though that is normally so. It may shine upon us in some turn of events or through another person; but anything that makes manifest is light and God is always behind it. For instance, a Christian may be reading in the privacy of his room the sort of magazine which one who belongs to the Lord should not be reading. He hears the footsteps of another Christian; the moment he hears a knock at the door, he quickly puts the magazine in a drawer and bids his friend come in. The coming of his friend is light, destined to reveal what he really is. His hiding of the magazine is darkness, designed to hide what he had been doing. When, however, under the conviction of the Holy Spirit, he confesses his sin to God (not only the sin of reading that sort of material, but the greater sin of hiding what he was doing), that is light again and upon his confession God forgives him his sin and cleanses him from all unrighteousness. Perhaps the Spirit might then guide him to share with his friend what has happened between himself and God.

We do not, however, need to quote hypothetical cases, for all of us have had experience in things small or great of the light shining and ourselves hiding, though we may not all know what it is to come into the light again — but we must do so, if we are to live in the Holiest.

It can be seen, then, that contrary to what many expect, the one in the Holiest is likely to know more conviction of sin rather than less, because the light there is so much brighter and he is becoming more sensitive to it. He will see things to be sin which he never saw to be such while he was only in the Holy Place. Instead of seeing himself less of a sinner, he will see himself more of one than ever and it is quite evident that repentance will have to be the habit of his soul, if he is to remain there.

This will in all probability be the case especially in his relationships with others. The nearer the spokes of a wheel get to the hub, the nearer they get to one another and that is when you can have trouble! Let us imagine two butterflies on neighboring spokes of a bicycle wheel, each making his way to the hub. For 50 percent of the way to the hub, they have no problems with each other, perhaps not for 95 percent of the way. It is in the last 5 percent of the way that they find their wings are touching, even clashing and each begins to react toward the other. They find they just cannot make that last 5 percent unless they do so together with folded wings.

There was a time in my Christian life when I did not seem to have problems in my relationships with others. I imagined I went through the world smiling at everybody, with everybody smiling back at me. There were problems, all right, but I was blissfully unaware of them. I was only in the Holy Place, only 75 percent, or at best, 95 percent of the way to the Hub. But when I wanted to get into the Holiest and go that last 5 percent, I found there were many things in my attitudes to others that needed my repentance and God's forgiveness, and I discovered that not everybody had been smiling at me; they had seen and noted and remembered the wrongs I had done and the wounds I had inflicted. And I had the humiliation of having to take the place of the wrong one on this, that, and the other matter, as I entered the Holiest.

Even while we are only in the Holy Place, enough light gets through to us to show us what is wrong in that last 5 percent. An unwillingness here is what hinders us from getting in. What brings revival is going that last 5 percent of the way. And when we have entered by grace into the Holiest, it will be on this 5 percent that the light will continue to shine. It is here that things can so easily go wrong again and where we need the constant restorations of grace. And the Holy Spirit will reveal it all in the white light of the Holiest and apply the remedy.

This brings us to the second feature of life in the Holiest; it is that there in the midst of the all-revealing light the blood of Jesus Christ, God's Son, cleanses us from all sin and that continuously. In the center of the Holiest lay the ark with the mercy seat upon it. The cherubim of glory fashioned out of it overshadowed that seat with their wings and were looking down upon the blood stains left there by successive sprinklings of the blood of sin-offerings. The only previous mention of those cherubim in the Bible is in Genesis — where we read that they were placed at the east of the Garden of Eden with a flaming sword, turning every way to keep the way of the tree of life. Now, however, the sword has been sheathed and they look down with wonder at the blood, a symbol of the way God has devised to bring guilty man back to Himself.

We have already seen the ark as picturing the Lord Jesus; it was made of acacia wood, overlaid within and without with gold, symbolizing His humanity and Deity; and the tables of the law were within, for He is the embodiment of the holy law of God. And yet on top of that law and indeed, based upon it, is the mercy seat sprinkled with blood, telling us that our many infringements of that law have been anticipated and settled by Jesus on the cross. So it is that the mercy offered us in the Holiest is a mercy sprinkled with blood; and this gives the guilty conscience peace and takes away its stain.

> My God to know that Thou art just
> Gives rest and peace within;
> I could not in a mercy trust
> That takes no count of sin.

But this mercy *has* taken account of sin and that in the most awesome way possible, by the Son of God bearing its judgment on the cross.

> Jehovah bade His sword awake,
> O Christ it woke 'gainst Thee;
> Thy blood the flaming blade must slake,
> Thy heart its sheath must be.
> All for my sake, my peace to make,
> Now sleeps that sword for me.

And this mercy seat, this Lord Jesus, stands waiting for us right in the midst of the Shekinah glory. The sight of His blood sprinkled there "wins the guilty to be bold" and we come, for the promise is "If we walk in the light, as he is in the light, we have fellowship one with another, and the blood of Jesus Christ, his Son, cleanseth us from all sin" (1 John 1:7).

I used to think that this verse must have things the wrong way around (what temerity to think such of Holy Scripture!), that it should have read, "If we are cleansed from sin, then we can walk in the light." But walking in the light comes first, because it is only as I permit the light to show me up that I see where I need to be cleansed. There in the Holiest whatever the light reveals, the blood of Jesus cleanses as I say yes to Him. Indeed, if we are willing to say yes immediately, we may regard ourselves as not having left the Holiest at all. It is not a life of being in and out of the Holiest all the time. There in the Holiest of All the light is shining and the blood is cleansing continually. It is only the stiff neck that will not bow the head and call sin, sin that puts us back into the Holy Place. Saying yes to the light is part of life in the Holiest, and forgiveness and cleansing always follow.

We must, however, learn to exercise faith in the power of the blood of Jesus, or else we will find that all-revealing light more than we can bear. The simple truth is that we cannot be whiter to the eye of God and more at peace with Him than what the blood of Jesus makes us when we repent. David seems to have caught sight of that when he prayed, "Wash me and I shall be whiter than snow" (Ps. 51:7). There is nothing we know of which is whiter than snow. No advertiser of a detergent would dare to claim for his product that it makes things even as white as snow, much less whiter than snow. But here David, one of the most defiled sinners in the Bible, says, "If God washes me, I shall be whiter than snow." What a place to be brought into! Grace brings us into a better position than that from which Adam fell. In the days of Adam's innocence, he was as white as snow; the blood of Jesus, however, makes us *whiter* than snow, which is something better than the restoration of innocence. That we have lost forever, but we are given something better — purity by the blood of Jesus. Jesus did not say, "Blessed are the innocent in heart," but "Blessed are the pure in heart." And the pure in heart are those who, although they have lost their innocence, "have washed their robes and made them white in the blood of the Lamb" (Rev. 7:14). And this purity by the blood of Jesus is better and safer than innocence, which at best is a very fragile thing.

And what else is in the Holiest? There we pass from the shadow Christian life to the substance. All three persons of the Trinity become real to us in a way They never were in the Holy Place: indeed, all three have come to live in us. Familiar truths that have long since gone stale on us in the Holy Place, such as the love of God, the majesty of God, the salvation of God, the cross of Christ, the hope of heaven, and so on dawn on us in a new and awesome reality and we worship Him as we never did before. Our service ceases to be the mechanical thing it had become, just ritual duties, but is now the overflow of full hearts. Sometimes in the Holiest there are occasions when more than usually we are given such sights of Jesus and His grace for sinners that we feel we could shout for joy, or weep for love, or prostrate ourselves before Him in adoration. I only know when I have looked at a meeting from the platform on those occasions when the Lord has visited us, faces have shone like the sun, and as we have sung, it looked as if some were about to take off for glory! The Shekinah was upon us.

These are perhaps special times in the Holiest; more often we must walk by faith, just letting the peace of God rule in our hearts (Col. 3:15), that is, letting that peace be the arbitrator, and when it is disturbed by something of self or sin, coming to Jesus for cleansing and daring to count on Him for the supply of what we confess we lack of holiness. And this walking by faith is just as much substance and not shadow as those other times when we have more conscious experiences of His glory, for as the eleventh chapter of this epistle says, "Faith is the substance of things hoped for" (11:1). One who has such faith does not wait for feelings, but treats things hoped for as fact because God has promised, and acting on them finds them become substance.

Nowhere outside of Scripture is the Holiest of All better described than in the words of T. Binney's famous hymn:

> Eternal Light! Eternal Light!
>   How pure the soul must be,
> When, placed within Thy searching sight,
> It shrinks not, but with calm delight,
>   Can live and look on Thee!
>
> The spirits that surround Thy throne
>   May bear the burning bliss;
> But that is surely theirs alone,
> Since they have never, never known,
>   A fallen world like this.
>
> O, how shall I, whose native sphere
>   Is dark, whose mind is dim,
> Before the Ineffable appear,
> And on my naked spirit bear
>   The uncreated beam?

There is a way for man to rise
    To that sublime abode:
An Offering and a Sacrifice,
A Holy Spirit's energies,
    An Advocate with God.

These, these prepare us for the sight
    Of holiness above:
The sons of ignorance and night
May dwell in the eternal light,
    Through the eternal love!

Entering Into the
Holiest

Having therefore, brethren, boldness to enter into the holiest by the blood of Jesus,
> by a new and living way, which he hath consecrated for us, through the veil, that is to say, his flesh;

and having an high priest over the house of God;
> let us draw near
> with a true heart
> in full assurance of faith,
> having our hearts sprinkled from an evil conscience,
> and our bodies washed with pure water.

— Hebrews 10:19-22

6

Entering Into the
Holiest

HAVING SEEN THE contrast between living in the Holy
Place and living in the Holiest, we must now ask ourselves how
we in practice pass from the one to the other. This is precisely
the subject of the verses we are considering (10:19-22). They
call us to appropriate what has been provided and enter into
the Holiest, and they tell us how in the simplest terms.

The form of the words is the language of appropriation:
"having . . . , let us. . . ," words which are used in other
places when this is the subject. In 2 Corinthians 7:1 we have
the same sort of phrases: "Having therefore these promises . . .
let us. . . ." And earlier in Hebrews (4:14-16), we have it again:
"Seeing we have a great high priest . . . , let us. . . ." It is the call
to act on what we have, and in this way we will find we pass
from shadow to substance in our Christian experience.

BOLDNESS THROUGH THE BLOOD

In the particular verses we are considering, we are urged
to enter in on the basis of two things we are told we have. The
first is boldness: "Having therefore, brethren, boldness to
enter into the holiest through the blood of Jesus. . . ." I have

asked myself if the apostle's meaning is that I enter through the
blood of Jesus, or that I have boldness through the blood of
Jesus to enter. There is a difference. After careful consideration, I am convinced that the latter is meant — we have
boldness through the blood of Jesus. We enter through the
new and living way, but we have boldness to enter that way by
His blood. Andrew Murray says in writing on this passage,
"The boldness with which we are told to enter is not, first of all,
a conscious feeling of confidence; it is the objective right and
liberty of entrance of which the blood assures us. The measure
of our boldness is the measure of the worth God attaches to the
blood of Jesus."

That this boldness is basically objective rather than subjective is proved by the use of the word *therefore;* "having
therefore, brethren, boldness. . . ." It is based on all that he has
already said of the power of that blood to bring Jesus into the
Holiest (He who was laden with more sins than any one of us
and yet was able to enter by that blood) and of its power to
cleanse our consciences from dead works to serve the living
God — we shall elaborate on the latter in the next chapter.
However, the more immediate context of that word *therefore*
is the verses that tell us that "this man, after he had offered one
sacrifice for sins forever, sat down . . . ," and that in this He was
unlike the earthly priests who offered continually the same
sacrifices that could never take away sins, whose work was
never finished and who therefore could never sit down; but He
"by one offering hath perfected forever them that are sanctified." That section is capped by the words "their sins and
their iniquities will I remember no more; now where remission
of these is there is no more offering for sin," and this immediately precedes the verse with our "therefore." That shows
clearly enough on what our boldness to enter is based — the
one sacrifice for sins forever, what is often called "the finished
work of Christ." One verse of the hymn "There is life for a look"
is a perfect commentary on this:

> Then doubt not thy welcome, since God has declared
>   There remaineth no more to be done,
> That once in the end of the age He appeared
>   And completed the work He begun.

This bold liberty to enter in is especially for the one who feels that because of sin and failure he has no such right. If it was written that we have boldness to enter through our victorious life, or our constant walk with the Lord, or our loving attitude to others, or our unfailing purity, then he surely would not qualify, for he would be the first to say he had not achieved these things as he should. But it is boldness by the blood of Jesus which is spoken of here and the blood is for sin and nothing else. Therefore it is assumed that the people who are offered this boldness to enter are sinners and failing saints. Therefore not even their sins can deprive them of this boldness if they confess them, for they were all anticipated and settled in that precious blood long ago.

Dear diffident one, you feel yourself a second-rate Christian; yes, you are, but grace offers you, as a railroad conductor once offered the people in his overcrowded train, "a first-class seat for second-class passengers." Believe, then, that there is given you, just as you are, this objective boldness to enter the Holiest by the blood, and as you believe, it will become a strong subjective confidence, and you will come and take your seat.

Some time ago my wife and I were praying together and I asked God with some warmth for spiritual enlargement for myself, that I might be more this and more that — a real prayer of aspiration, if ever there was one. It came to me afterwards that in so doing I was trying unwittingly to enter the Holiest by some other way than that of the blood. I asked myself whether, if something along the lines of my prayer had immediately happened to me, I would have felt I had more boldness to enter: I saw that had indeed been my attitude in a subtle way, though frankly I had not been expecting much to happen. Then the Lord said to me, "But you already have in the blood of Jesus the fullest boldness to enter, without any of the qualities you have been asking Me for!" Then He showed me something deeper. I had not come by the blood of Jesus because I did not want to be seen as a beggar again at the back door, confessing I lacked all these things and had nothing. Beware of these prayers of aspiration! Sometimes they can be a side-stepping of the place of confession; sometimes they can be like a beggar coming to the front door, as if he was not a beggar, when he should have been going to the back door — a door which he will find is open for him all the time. Boldness by the blood of Jesus is a boldness that even a beggar may have. That being so, the sooner and oftener we confess that is what we are and that we lack everything, the more we will enjoy this boldness as something right within our reach.

Boldness or liberty to enter the Holiest, then, is the first thing we have.

OUR HIGH PRIEST

Then, secondly, we read, " . . . having a high priest over the house of God." The "therefore" that applies to our boldness also applies to this phrase. Paul refers here to all he has already said about Jesus as our high priest, not only our Aaron, but our Melchizedek, which we have dealt with in a previous chapter. As we approach the Holiest, we are to recognize that He is already there for us. Yes, there for us, having been tried as we are tried, having been compassed about with weakness as we are, and therefore able to bear gently with the ignorant and erring, and "touched with the feeling of our infirmities" (4:15). Beautiful word, *touched!* When you are really touched by another's situation of need, you wipe the tear from your eye; so does Jesus in the Holiest, as we seek to approach. He knows our struggles with our earthly mindedness and unspiritual disposition; He knows our longings to enter and yet our inability really to grasp all our teachers have told us. So often in the time of our greatest need our notes of the wonderful addresses we have heard are not around! Then it is that our High Priest in the Holiest stretches out His hand to us and says in effect, "I have heard your sighs and seen your struggles; don't be concerned too much about your teachers, and certainly don't spend any time looking for those notes; here, take My hand," and the next moment we are in, we know not how! We are not at all sure that we have taken the right steps in the right order, or that we have prayed the right prayer in the right words. But it does not seem to matter too much to Jesus. A sigh seems to be enough; in any case, we had not strength for much more. But His loving hand drew us into the Holiest; if there is more to learn about it all, we can learn it in there with Him.

Learn, then, to avail yourself of your High Priest and to expect such treatment from Him. Nothing touches Him so much as acknowledged weakness. That being so, we can afford to confess to Him what we are. Let the words "and having a high priest over the house of God" be like a sweet morsel in your mouth.

Having these two things, we are told, "Let us draw near." While the veil still hung, it was saying, "Not yet; do not come near." But now that it has been rent in two and in view of what we are said to have, the word is a hearty "enter in." But let us not make it complicated here; entering in is nothing less than coming to Jesus, for He is both the One who brings us into blessing and the blessing itself.

A True Heart

The passage now goes on to describe the things that accompany a genuine coming to Jesus and are implied in the nature of the case. There are four such.

First we are told to draw near "with a true heart." This is not necessarily a good heart (if that were so, we would find ourselves asking, "How good?" and "Is ours good enough?"), but with a true heart, which is a heart that does not hide from the truth, but is honest about itself before God. Just such a man, presumably, was Nathanael, of whom Jesus said, "Behold, an Israelite indeed, in whom is no guile" (John 1:47). That did not mean that he was a man in whom there was no sin, but a man in whom there was no hiding of sin, who did not try to deceive himself and God about his condition. He knew he was confused and in the dark on many matters and the inference is he owned it to God. Perhaps that is what was going on "under the fig tree," where Jesus says He saw him, and because of which Jesus described him as without guile. This is the true heart with which we must come to Jesus.

This means in practice that, instead of just asking to be brought into the Holiest, we start by confessing we are not in it at all and "make no bones" about how we are. The major part of asking God for something is surely to confess we have not got it; why otherwise ask God for it if it is something we have? And if we do not have it, let us admit that fact to God and do so fully and deeply. God would much rather hear us confess that we are not in the Holiest than have us continually beseech Him to bring us there, for such asking may have no self-humbling about it and may be covering up our real state. But if we are honest enough to confess that as of now we are not there (no matter whether or not we have been there previously), He will certainly see to bringing us in. That being so, we can make the confession of our condition restfully and in depth, knowing that that very condition makes us candidates for the grace of God.

This extraordinary procedure goes for other aspects of the Christian life too: The way to become a Christian is to confess to God that you are not one; the way to be filled with the Holy Spirit is to confess you are empty; the way to be victorious in a matter is to be honest and confess you are defeated there; and the way into the Holiest is to confess you are only in the Holy Place. The way to enter the positive is to confess the negative, and it is the heart that is willing to do this honestly that is the true heart. Humbling, yes, but it is the way in *every* time.

FULL ASSURANCE OF FAITH

The confession of a true heart is effective only if it is made in full assurance of faith — that is, as mentioned in a previous chapter, faith in grace. This means that we see the very lack we confess constitutes our one qualification to be blessed, for the grace of God by its very nature specializes in people in our condition. When such faith in grace is clearly expressed to Jesus, it means that He has another case on His hands, and He does not fail.

We must, however, be fully assured that this is so, and that full assurance is only by faith, not by feelings. Many have wanted to come in full assurance of feeling, and if they do not feel these things as they imagine others do, they have despaired. Faith is that attitude which, even in the absence of all compatible feelings, dares to believe that the grace of God and the blood of Christ is sufficient for our need right now, just because God says so. God always responds to this and fulfills "the work of faith with power" (2 Thess. 1:11); peace and liberty follow.

THE HEART SPRINKLED

The third thing which must be true of us as we enter the Holiest is that we have "our hearts sprinkled from an evil conscience." Reference to any concordance will show that the word *sprinkled* in the Old Testament is used in nearly every case in connection with the sprinkling of sacrificial blood on persons or objects. This use of the word is carried over into the New Testament, for we read in Hebrews 12:24 that we are come "to Jesus . . . and to the blood of sprinkling that speaketh better things than that of Abel." The use of the term "the blood of sprinkling" can only mean, as I see it, that it is blood *for* sprinkling, i.e., blood for the purpose of being applied whenever needed.

This certainly comes out in the first reference to the sprinkling of blood in the Old Testament. In the story of the Passover lamb in Exodus 12, each householder first shed the blood of a lamb and then sprinkled it on the doorposts of his house. The blood had to be applied; any household which omitted doing so failed to experience its efficacy in the hour of Egypt's judgment, for it was only when God saw the blood that He passed over them. There was a big difference that night between the blood shed and the blood sprinkled, as there is in Christian experience today. It is not enough for the blood of Christ to be shed on Calvary; it has to be sprinkled, that is, applied to our sinful hearts and to the specific sins that are accusing us and producing in us an evil conscience.

This, then, is what is in view in the words "having our hearts sprinkled from an evil conscience," sprinkled, that is, with the blood of Jesus. The power of His blood is such as to make us "perfect as pertaining to the conscience." What a perfection to enjoy right now! If there is still something condemning you in your heart, agree with God about it and confess it, before you think of entering the Holiest. Direct the full assurance of faith, about which we have spoken, to the stain in question and to the efficacy of the blood of Jesus to cleanse it, and be at peace. Ask yourself which is greater — your sin, or the blood of Jesus. There can be only one answer.

> Oft as it is sprinkled
> On our guilty hearts,
> Satan in confusion,
> Terror-struck, departs.

THE BODY WASHED

The fourth matter mentioned here is that we are to have "our bodies washed with pure water." This expression must refer to the fact that it was necessary for Aaron to wash his flesh in water at the brazen laver before he entered the Holiest on the great Day of Atonement (Lev. 16:4). It seems that the heart represents the inner life, at the center of which stands the conscience, and the body represents the outer life with its various activities and relationships.

Now the inner life, the heart and conscience, is not said to be washed with water; it has to be sprinkled with blood. As the hymn says,

> Crimson do my sins seem to me,
> Water cannot wash them away.

Tears of repentance cannot remove those stains, and not even in itself "the washing of water by the word" (Eph. 5:26). They need blood. The reading of the Word of God has a cleansing effect only as it provokes us to self-judgment and leads us to the blood of Christ.

But the outer life, that is a different matter. Here the water of a practical, specific, down-to-earth repentance is very much a necessity, a repentance that is not only toward God but toward others, where that is needed. This will have to be expressed in a conscientious renunciation of present wrongs and restitution for past ones, as the occasion may require and as God guides. In this way the outer life is cleaned up.

However, the doing of these things is nonetheless under grace and not under law. Just so was it in the case of Zacchaeus.

When Jesus went into the house alone with Zacchaeus, there were doubtless confessions made to Him, provoked by the very grace of His coming into the house at all. And Zacchaeus's heart, his inner life, was cleansed from an evil conscience by the forgiveness of the Son of man. As a result, he spontaneously announced his intention in the hearing of the crowd to pay back four times what he had wrongly taken from people and to give half his goods to the poor, and there and then he set off to do so. He really repented in style, that man; but it was all grace! In this way both his inner and his outer life were cleansed, or to use the language of these verses in Hebrews, he had his heart sprinkled from an evil conscience and his body washed with pure water.

Do not, however, delay your coming into the Holiest until you have got all these things straight. It is not always possible to deal with everything immediately, but God accepts your intention to obey and you can come now. Indeed, the doing of some of these things will need the reinforcements of grace which are only to be found when you are in the Holiest. Furthermore, it often happens that a person realizes where his outer life needs to be cleaned up only when he has begun to walk in the light with Jesus.

Just one thought before we pass on. Sometimes we hear the phrase "living within the veil." There is, for instance, a devotional hymn each verse of which begins with "Within the veil," and another hymn which speaks of being shut in with God. The truth is there is no veil now to be within and we must never speak as if there is, for that which shuts some in, shuts others out. The Holiest is open to all. There is no "ingroup" and if you should ever feel there is and that you are not part of it, you may need to repent of jealousy or excessive sensitiveness and to tell yourself that you cannot be more "in" than what the blood of Jesus brings you when you take the sinner's place.

In any case, this entering into the Holiest is not a once-for-all step which some having taken, maintains them there "for keeps." What we have before us here is simply the choice we must face again and again between two levels of Christian experience; now that we have come to know Christ, are we going to live our Christian lives in the Holy Place or in the Holiest of All? And inasmuch as it is easy to slip back into something short of the Holiest, we cannot choose today for tomorrow. We can only choose the Holiest as each day and each issue arises. And the comforting thing for all of us is that in no matter what new state of need we may find ourselves, that place of most intimate proximity to God which we call the Holiest is always available to us and if we are content with nothing less, we may have boldness by the blood to enter there again and live there.

So, in the words of the title of a book which Bunyan wrote after he had at last seen the grace of God, *"Come and welcome to Jesus."*

The Power of the
Blood of Christ

But Christ being come an high priest of good things to come, by a greater and more perfect tabernacle, not made with hands, that is to say, not of this building; neither by the blood of goats and calves,

but by his own blood he entered in once into the holy place, having obtained eternal redemption for us.

For if the blood of bulls and goats, and the ashes of an heifer sprinkling the unclean, sanctifieth to the purifying of the flesh:

how much more shall the blood of Christ, who through the eternal Spirit offered himself without spot to God, purge your conscience from dead works to serve the living God?

— Hebrews 9:11-14

7

The Power of the
Blood of Christ

SO MUCH IS said in the Epistle to the Hebrews of the blood
of Jesus and we ourselves have reiterated this term so often in
these pages, that it would be well to pause and inquire as to its
real meaning and how it is that it accomplishes so much for us,
lest it be considered just a cliché used only by a minority of
Christians. We should be aware that to many people, even to
believers, constant use of the term is offensive and they would
much prefer to speak about the death of Christ or the cross of
Christ. Fair enough, it could be regarded as a meaningless
cliché if we never explained the special significance that Scripture attaches to the expression. The fact is that "the death of
Christ," "the cross of Christ," and "the blood of Christ" are not
interchangeable terms, and if God in certain contexts speaks
about the blood of His Son, it is because that phrase expresses
certain aspects of truth the others do not. Each has its special
meaning and emphasis.

The purpose of this chapter, however, is not merely to
inform the mind as to Scripture terminology, nor even to
remove certain intellectual stumbling blocks. We are concerned rather with how things work out in practice and the

truth in this chapter might prove to be to the reader the most liberating part of the whole book and provide him with wings with which to soar to God in praise and gratitude.

There is a short paragraph in the ninth chapter of this epistle which explains more clearly than any other the meaning of the blood of Christ and how it is so mightily operative on our behalf. Verses 13 and 14 read in the King James Version: "For if the blood of bulls and of goats, and the ashes of an heifer sprinkling the unclean, sanctifieth to the purifying of the flesh: how much more shall the blood of Christ, who through the eternal Spirit offered himself without spot to God, purge your conscience from dead works to serve the living God?" The word *purge* implies a rather drastic operation, involving scrubbing and much else. Actually it is simply the old English word for "cleanse," and the same Greek word is more usually so translated even in the King James Version. The subject here, then, is the cleansing of the conscience from dead works by the blood of Christ and the theme thus follows on from our previous chapter where we spoke of "having our hearts sprinkled from an evil conscience." The passage illustrates the meaning and operation of the blood of Christ by referring us back to an Old Testament ritual where the ashes of a heifer were sprinkled upon a man who had become ceremonially defiled. I myself have found this reference to the ashes of a heifer enormously helpful, for it typifies to me the meaning of the blood of Christ more clearly than any other type. The day its meaning dawned on me, I walked around my study, saying, "Ashes, ashes, the ashes of a heifer sprinkling the unclean — I see it all!"

Before going on to expound this phrase, let us pause to note that this verse speaks of the conscience and implies that it is sometimes defiled; otherwise, why should it speak of it being cleansed? Conscience is the most inexorable faculty within us. It speaks to us of what is right and tells us where we have done wrong; and sin always leaves a legacy of guilt upon it — what the hymn writers so often call "the stain of sin." Long after a sin has ceased to occupy the thoughts, and long after it has ceased to grip the heart and even when it has faded almost from the memory, the stain of it still remains upon the conscience, giving the soul a sense of guilt and defilement. The passage of time does nothing to remove the stain of that guilt. Indeed, it is rather like the stains in a cup we have failed to wash. Perhaps we were too tired to wash the cup in which we had had some coffee before retiring to bed. In the morning we see the cup there; the coffee has gone, but the stains remain. If we leave it for a day, they are still there. If we leave it for weeks and months, the stains remain. Even so the defilement on the conscience abides long after the sin has ceased. Indeed, in view of its ongoing legacy, it has not ceased at all; it is still active in accusing our consciences.

What an extraordinary faculty this thing called conscience is within us! When it is defiled, it can make us miserable in heart, unwell in body, ill at ease with our fellows, and certainly cut off from God. Of course, there are differences in sensitivity of conscience between one man and another, as there are differences in scales. Some scales are designed to weigh the largest bulks and will not register anything less than a hundredweight; on the other hand, there are scales in our laboratories so sensitive that they will register the weight of a postage stamp, or much less. In the same way, some people's consciences register only when they have done something that will involve them with the police; there are others for whom the least omission registers as guilt. It might be regarded as a questionable blessing to have a conscience as sensitive as that, but unless we have a conscience sensitized and instructed by the Holy Spirit, how are we to know what it is that has gone wrong between us and God and seek the remedy that God has provided?

Dead Works

Before proceeding to the remedy, we must notice that what the blood of Christ cleanses our conscience from is not so much sin as what the verse calls "dead works." The New Testament speaks of three sorts of works. It speaks, first of all, of wicked works (Col. 1:21). It is not difficult for us to know what they are: straight-down-the-line sin. Then, there are good works; these are not random good deeds, but rather "good works that God hath before ordained that we should walk in them" (Eph. 2:10), that sphere of service for Himself and others that He has planned for us. Then, there are "dead works," something between wicked works and good works. It is important for us to know what is meant by this term.

The definition I would give is that dead works are the things we feel we ought to do to become better Christians, but which we have never quite succeeded in doing. It would be interesting to pass around to a group of Christians a sheet of paper for each to write down the things he thinks he ought to do to become a better Christian and to be more used of God. What would we find on such a list? Perhaps that we ought to give ourselves more to prayer; that we ought to have more faith and confidence in God; that we ought to spend more time reading our Bibles; that we ought to have more caring for others; that we ought to manifest more holiness and patience; that we ought to have greater readiness to witness; and so the list could go on — ought, ought, ought. Of course, this might remain only a list on a sheet of paper for some. But if we try seriously to put these things into practice, we find ourselves facing a problem — we never quite succeed in doing them. There is nothing wrong with the standards that we espouse — "the commandment is holy and just and good" (Rom. 7:12) — but the trouble is that we seem to be unable to do them as they ought to be done.

What an impasse we are in! We are quite sure what will make us better Christians, but we are never able to fulfill the conditions. The result is that our failure to do these things only burdens our consciences and we end up with a greater sense of condemnation than before. Many Christians are going round with consciences condemned by the prayers they have not prayed, the promises they have not kept, the time they have not spent with their Bibles, the souls they have not witnessed to, the holy lives they have not lived, etc., etc. The attempt to do these works is so often dead and heavy, with no breath of the Spirit about them; while the failure to do them is deadlier still, for they only add to our sense of guilt.

Moreover, there is sometimes an unsuspected deceitfulness about dead works, which makes them especially offensive to God. We are often attempting by their means to regain what we have actually lost by our sin. If we are not in fellowship with God, it is not because we have not done this or that enough, but because of sin; and works, no matter how sincerely attempted, are no substitute for repentance and coming to the Cross; and in any case, as we have said, we shall inevitably fail to do them as they should be done.

These, I suggest, are what is meant by dead works; these are what burden the conscience; these are what prevent us entering the Holiest of All. But it is from just such a burden that the blood of Christ cleanses the conscience. It might be suggested that if one is not experiencing this in the Christian life, one is not experiencing anything.

THE ASHES OF A HEIFER

Now we are in a position to consider the blood of Christ as typified by this strange figure, the ashes of a heifer. The reference is to an ordinance set out in Numbers 19, where the ashes of a heifer mingled with water were sprinkled upon the ceremonially defiled one, in order to restore him to his privileges of worship in Israel. Under the law of Moses, anyone who had had contact with death was regarded as ceremonially unclean and excluded from certain privileges of worship until he was cleansed. To have touched a dead body, even a bone, or to have tended a man who died was enough to render a person defiled. And inasmuch as in the forty years in the wilderness a whole generation was dying out, all of whom had to be buried, people were all the time being defiled by death and excluded from their privileges. It was necessary, therefore, that there should be a mode of cleansing which was as continuously available as the defilement was continuously contracted. The high priest was ordered, therefore, to slay a red heifer, sprinkle its blood in the tabernacle, and burn its body outside the camp, reducing it to ashes, which ashes were then carefully preserved, barrels of them. Whenever a man knew he had been defiled, he would go to another who was "clean" and ask him to perform the cleansing ceremony upon him. That man would take a little bit of those ashes, mingle them with running water, and sprinkle them upon the unclean. He would do it again the seventh day, and after that the man was clean and could return to his religious privileges.

There is much more deeply significant detail in this ceremony which we need not go into here. My purpose is to fix your attention on the words "the ashes of an heifer," for they are, as I say, an illustration of what is meant by the blood of Jesus Christ. You cannot burn ashes, they are burned already. Ashes are what is left when the fire has done its work and are a memorial to that work. At Calvary the fire of the anger of God against human sin fell on the Son of God. One of the Psalms asks the question, "Who knoweth the power of thine anger?" (90:11). The only One who has known the full power of the anger of God against sin was Jesus Christ as He hung on the cross; and He not only knew it, He exhausted it. In Him the fire burnt itself out. That is something of what He meant when He uttered the words "It is finished." It was only after those words that the Roman soldier came and pierced His side and immediately blood and water came out. The blood of Jesus is a memorial to a fire that has finished its work and gone out. In other words, it is a token of His finished work, of judgment which has been exhausted by Him on our behalf. As we look at the blood of Jesus, all we see of that judgment are but the ashes of it. To that work the sinner need not add anything to put himself right with God; everything has been done for him. And the sprinkling of the ashes on the unclean betokens the application of the finished work of Christ to the guilty conscience, as the defiled one repents and believes. It is not enough for us to believe in the blood and preach the blood, we must personally apply the blood, and that can be humbling. But when we do so, the conscience is immediately cleansed, not only from sin, but from dead works.

See how this deliverance from dead works takes place. If His work for me is finished, as the blood declares it to be, it means that in one bound Jesus brings me into that fellowship with God that I had been striving for. What I was attempting to find by my works, I find as a gift at the foot of the cross. This in turn means that I am relieved of the painful obligation of seeking it in those other ways, and am set free from the condemnation they only succeeded in bringing me. If you had lost a one-pound note, or a five-dollar bill, and were looking everywhere for it, what would be the first thing you would do when you found it? Obviously, you would stop looking for it! And the first thing I do when I have found peace and fullness at the foot of the cross is to stop looking for it in other ways. This is freedom indeed. It was this that Bunyan was referring to when he described in *Pilgrim's Progress* a burden rolling off Pilgrim's back when he saw the cross. It was surely not merely the burden of sin that he lost that day, but much more the burden of dead works. It is this burden that Jesus is referring to, when He says, "Come unto me all ye that labour and are heavy laden and I will give you rest."

The burnt ashes and the shed blood, then, speak of the same thing, of a judgment that is finished. The blood of the lamb sprinkled on the doorposts on the Passover night uttered the same message. God had said that in the midst of the judgment which was coming on every house, "the blood shall be to you for a token." A token of what? A token that judgment had already come to the house on which it was sprinkled. It had come to the house when, as the sun was setting that evening, father and son slew the lamb and sprinkled the blood on the doorpost. The father had said to his son who, I imagine, hated to kill the little creature, "Either this lamb dies or you do." So it was that the judgment that otherwise would have fallen on the son fell on the lamb and the sprinkled blood on the doorpost was a token of that fact. Therefore solid peace was theirs, for judgment could not again visit that house.

Now this is something of which the blood of Jesus speaks in a way that the Cross of Jesus does not. The Cross speaks of something else — His unspeakable humiliations and His willingness to undergo them all for us. As we stand beneath the Cross, we see that our sins brought Him there, and that humbles us to repentance. But the blood symbolizes His words "It is finished," and it speaks only of the victory that has been won for us there. The hymns about the Cross, the Good Friday ones, are rightly solemn as they recall the brokenness of the Deity. But by a divine instinct the writers of hymns about the blood of Jesus invariably make them triumphant, joyful, and even rhythmic — some would think irreverently so! But that is altogether fitting — when the saints see the blood again and their liberty in that blood, you just cannot stop them rejoicing with loud praises and shining eyes and sometimes (don't be shocked!) with clapping hands; for the blood speaks of a victory that has been won for them, a judgment that has been spent, and a heart that has been delivered from dead works to serve the living God.

Yes, that is the final thing of which this verse speaks — when the conscience is cleansed from dead works, we are really free to serve the living God. Service for God and others, service that once was so dead, now flows as a simple consequence of knowing the way of conscious release through His blood. Service now is done "in newness of spirit and not in the oldness of the letter," not as a duty by means of which we hope to inherit blessing, but simply because we have already received it as a gift at the feet of Jesus, and we pour out our service in gratitude to Him. Prayer, study of the Word, devotion, caring for others, witnessing to the world, are done out of a full heart, cleansed by the blood, set free from the bondage of law, and actuated now by love for Him. There are no rules here, for there comes into our lives and service a joyous spontaneity.

Let us then be those who have constant recourse to the ever-available blood of Jesus and enjoy life in the Holiest, "having our hearts sprinkled from an evil conscience." As Charles Wesley wrote:

> Oh, may the least omission pain
> My well-instructed soul,
> And drive me to the blood again
> That makes the wounded whole.

The Alternative to
Going On — Drawing Back

Cast not away therefore your confidence which hath great recompense of reward. For ye have need of patience, that, after ye have done the will of God, ye might receive the promise.

For yet a little while, and he that shall come will come and will not tarry. Now the just shall live by faith; but if any man draw back, my soul shall have no pleasure in him.

But we are not of them who draw back unto perdition; but of them that believe to the saving of the soul.

— Hebrews 10:35-39

8

The Alternative to
Going On — Drawing Back

WE COME NOW to the solemn warning notes that sound all the way through the great epistle. After almost every unfolding of the sweet provisions of mercy there are inserted warnings as to the consequences of not embracing that mercy but of turning back. The emphasis of the epistle seems to be that, if we do not go on from shadow to substance as outlined in our previous chapters, we are not likely to remain standing still; going back is seen to be the only alternative to going on and that is serious indeed. The Christian life is like riding a bicycle; if you do not go on, you lose your balance and come off. The Christian's only safety is in going on, first from sin to grace and then from grace to further grace. But the possibility of not doing so is all the time there. And so we have the solemn warning passages in the epistle, and all along this one line — the danger of not going on further into grace but turning back into sin.

This we find even in chapter 10 of all chapters, the very peak of the whole epistle. The same passage that says, "Let us draw near" into the Holiest (10:22), also warns us of the possibility of "drawing back unto perdition" (10:39). The contrast between the alternatives is really quite shocking. On the one hand, we see the Holiest opened and that for the weakest and most unworthy; on the other, we see hell opened and the judgment of those who "tread underfoot the Son of God" more starkly described than anywhere else in Scripture. And the very ones who are so lovingly urged to enter the Holiest by the blood of Jesus are apparently capable of refusing to do so and "drawing back to perdition."

It is the phrase "to perdition" that puzzles us. We can understand a professing Christian's standing still in his Christian life and not progressing. But if it is true that in the Christian life there is no standing still, then we can understand a man slipping back. Who of us, as children of God, has not known something of backsliding in heart, if not in outward ways? But to "draw back to perdition," that is a puzzle indeed; this surely must be something more than backsliding. Here is something that we must come to grips with, and that not merely to explain it away. If there is a challenge to our hearts here, then we must understand its nature, expose ourselves to it, and benefit from it.

In order to clarify the apostle's teaching, let us ask certain questions in consecutive order. First, what is the turning back referred to in the epistle? It is expressed, as to its ultimate form by the phrase "departing from the living God" (3:12). A careful consideration of the relevant passages in the epistle leads me to the conclusion that this means that a man may ultimately, deliberately, and, as far as his intentions are concerned, finally rescind his faith in Christ and say in effect, "If there is such a thing as salvation, I don't want it, and if there is such a place as heaven, I don't want to go there." The word *depart* is always a very strong and decisive word. The same Greek word appears again in 2 Timothy 2:19: "Let every one that nameth the name of Christ depart from iniquity." We are not expected to depart from an iniquity slowly or by degrees, but decisively and, as far as our intentions are concerned, finally. In the same way, one can depart from the living God. The word appears also in 1 Timothy 4:1: "In the latter times some shall depart from the faith." Obviously, such a departure from the faith will be deliberate and decisive; it will be what we call apostasy. This word *apostasy* is an Anglicized Greek word and appears only once in this form in the Greek New Testament, in 2 Thessalonians 2:3, where we are told that the coming of the Lord will not take place, "except there come a falling away [apostasia] first," and the word means much the same as the "departing from the living God" in the Epistle to the Hebrews. This meaning is borne out by other forms of the same word: in Acts 21:21 (". . . thou teachest all the Jews that are among the Gentiles to *forsake* Moses") and in Matthew 5:31 ("Whosoever shall put away his wife, let him give her a writing of *divorcement*"). What we are presented with here is the danger of a professing Christian utterly repudiating his faith in Christ, that is, apostatizing.

In this situation we can only regard such a person as a Christ-rejector along with all those who have rejected the gospel offer and refused to confess Christ. Indeed, his rejection of Christ is far more culpable than theirs, because he actually has made a confession and knows so much more. If he is reminded of that earlier confession, he will probably deny the validity of it and tell us that as of now he wants nothing of salvation. We can then hardly do anything else than accept his word for it. If he says he wants nothing of salvation, how can we tell him he is going to have it nonetheless and end up in heaven, whether he likes it or not, just because he once made a profession of faith, the validity of which he now denies? No, he is now in the position of the Christ-rejector and cannot but share the eternal judgment of all such as long as he remains in that condition. But, thank God, he need not remain in that condition; he may begin to follow Christ — in a way that he had never done before. As we shall see in a later chapter, the condition of apostasy is not one from which there is no recovery. The door of mercy is still open. If he is a Christ-rejector, he has the privilege open to all such, that of entering that door, if he will but turn to the Lord from that far-off place. If blasphemous Saul of Tarsus entered, why not he? But the danger is that he may choose not to do so and that he will end his days in the place of an apostate.

It is not suggested that a professing Christian would come

to this place easily, suddenly, or even unexpectedly. Paul certainly does not charge his readers with having got there, but he does seem to suggest that they might set out on a road that would, if persistently followed, ultimately lead to it. So it is that he sets up flashing warning signs at that terrible end-of-the-road place. There is a sense in which this danger is only hypothetical in his thinking, for he says, "But, beloved, we are persuaded better things of you, and things that accompany salvation" (6:9). But hypothetical or not, it is a solemn danger nonetheless, and he warns them of at least two prior stages that could lead there.

First, he warns them of the danger of drift. No sooner has he opened his epistle with a majestic description of the greatness of the One by whom their salvation has come than he breaks off to fire his first warning shot across their bows: "Therefore we ought to give the more earnest heed to the things which we have heard, lest haply we drift from them" (2:1). Drifting is not something we do of set purpose; indeed, it is not anything we do at all; it just happens gradually, given certain conditions. Imagine a little rowboat drifting slowly out to sea without the fishermen in it realizing it. They are busy tending their lines and think they are stationary, just outside the harbor. But the offshore wind and the outgoing tide are causing the little boat gradually to drift farther and farther out to sea, where, if there is a sudden change of weather, they will be in grave peril. So may a person, once apparently near to God, gradually drift from Him and from His grace. The conditions in which this drift take place are not several, but basically just one — neglect of repentance. He has permitted himself to play with sin, perhaps only in small matters, in wrong attitudes if not in wrong acts, and he has failed to see the separation these cause between himself and God and to confess them. The offshore wind which is all the time blowing from the world helps to take him yet farther away. Then follow other things, which likewise are not repented of, and so the drift from God continues; it can be so gradual to the person concerned as to be almost imperceptible, at least at first.

The next stage is that of his becoming "hardened through

the deceitfulness of sin" (3:13). When God speaks to him, he hardens his heart, stiffens his neck, and justifies himself. He will not accept a challenge and admit himself to be at fault. He adopts this attitude because of the deceitfulness of sin, that is, because sin masks itself. He sees the other person's actions, but not his reactions. The other person may be wrong, but his reactions toward him are wrong too; indeed, in God's sight the latter are often far more culpable than the wrong of the other. Or, it may be that his compromises with the world are subtle and he is so much in the habit of rationalizing them that sin has deceived him; and so he hardens his heart against any reproof.

That condition of hardness can go on and on, become ever more chronic, until — until what? Until one day, the one concerned, when faced with, we will suppose, the threat of some intense anti-Christian persecution, permits himself to be pushed over the line into a complete disavowal of his faith, in order to spare himself. It was this sort of person the Lord Jesus had in mind when He said in Matthew 13:21, "When tribulation or persecution ariseth because of the word, by and by he is offended," or as the Revised Standard Version translates it, "immediately he falls away." Living in an apocalyptic age as we do, the tribulation and persecution referred to could be for the believer — let's face it — the concentration camp or the firing squad. In the light of such a threat, would a man who has long been drifting from God and has become hardened through the deceitfulness of sin be willing to suffer a martyr's death for the sake of Christ? If he has not been willing to deny self for Christ's sake when the going was comparatively easy, would he not be likely, now that faithfulness will prove so costly, to deny Christ for self's sake and thus lose his crown? (Rev. 2:11).

This is the way in which Paul envisages that the Hebrew Christians to whom he writes might reach that end-of-the-road place of apostasy. First, there is the gradual drifting from "the things that they had heard"; then the progressive hardening of their hearts through the deceitfulness of sin; and then the crucial test, the prospect of suffering and loss for Christ's sake and in that test a departing from the living God and a rescinding of their faith in order to spare themselves the cross. He makes it clear that he trusts it will never come to that and he bids them "call to remembrance the former days" when they had suffered so much (10:32) because of their acknowledgment of the One their nation had crucified. But if they were to go the whole way from the shadow to the substance and take their stand with Jesus outside the camp of Judaism (13:13), then they would have to bear His reproach in a far more acute way and would face the prospect of even more severe sufferings. Then it might be that the cold-in-heart would be in danger of apostatizing from Christ altogether and drawing back to their former Judaism.

It is in this connection we are to understand the words of Jesus: "He that shall endure to the end, the same shall be saved" (Matt. 24:13). This text is not intended to suggest that the believer will not know till the end whether he has qualified. If that were the case, he would be in doubt about his salvation all the time till then, thereby making it a matter of works rather than of grace. In the context the Lord is speaking of that time of "great tribulation, such as was not since the beginning of the world, no, nor ever shall be" (24:21), when Satan will seek especially to "wear out the saints of the most High" (Dan. 7:25) and when they will be hated of all men for the sake of Christ. Then the pressures on the believer to repudiate his faith altogether may well be immense. But the one who has truly learned to live by faith in his heavenly Melchizedek will be given grace to endure to the end without apostatizing and thus through faith in Christ will be saved.

Of course, it is not always the prospect of suffering and loss for Christ's sake that provides the final push into apostasy. For some, merely the blandishments of the world and the favors it offers are enough. If they cannot have both Christ and Barabbas, then they will choose Barabbas and, in effect, put Christ again on the cross.

It is because the alternative to going on is going back that one of Paul's oft-repeated injunctions in this epistle is that the Hebrew Christians should hold fast their profession of faith without wavering and not cast it away. Four times the phrase "hold fast" occurs: "if we hold fast the confidence and rejoicing of the hope firm unto the end" (3:6); "if we hold the beginning of our confidence fast unto the end" (3:14); "let us hold fast our profession" (4:14); "let us hold fast the profession of our faith without wavering; for he is faithful that promised" (10:23). And, as we have seen in a previous chapter, it is faith in the immutability of grace that we must hold fast, so that whenever sin becomes a part of our experience, we may not despair, but come again to the Lord. But Paul exhorts us not only to "hold fast," but above all to "go on" — to live in the Holiest and in the joys of the new covenant and much else — so that we shall be yet further removed from the processes of decline to which we have referred.

Let us make quite clear that what we have in view here is not merely backsliding, as normally understood, but a place right beyond backsliding. Moreover, we have been careful to use the phrase "the *professing* Christian," for he may turn out to have been only a professor, and not a possessor. The eternal security of the *true* believer remains untouched. There may be variations in such a person's walk with the Lord; the work of sanctification in his heart will never be complete till he gets to glory; but whatever his current condition, these words of Jesus are still true of him: "My sheep hear my voice, and I know them, and they follow me: and I give unto them eternal life; and they shall never perish, neither shall any man pluck them out of my hand" (John 10:27,28). This fact gives him every inducement to return to the Lord from even the most grievous backsliding. But this epistle warns us that there is a place right beyond that, an end-of-the-road place, where a man has utterly turned his back on Christ and has "trodden under foot the Son of God, and hath counted the blood of the covenant, wherewith he was sanctified, an unholy thing, and hath done despite unto the Spirit of grace" (10:29).

Whether such a person was ever a true Christian, born of the Spirit, in the first place is very much open to question. On the evidence we are certainly entitled to doubt it. This is a matter we shall deal with in detail in a later chapter.

A Yes-and-No Paradox

There is, however, a prior question we must answer first: Is it at all possible for a truly born-again one to apostatize in this way?

Here, it seems, the truth is finely balanced and we must be willing to accept one of the many paradoxes of Scripture. A paradox is an apparent contradiction; and in the following paragraphs in this and the next two chapters you will find statements that would almost seem to contradict one another. But they are there in Scripture nonetheless, in order to preserve the fine balance of the truth. When the Spirit Himself applies the truth to the heart, there is never any confusion, for He presents first one aspect and then another according to our need at the moment, and it is all for "the perfecting of the saints." It is only when we try to systematize things too much that we cause confusion and questioning in peoples' minds.

In reply, then, to the question whether a child of God can apostatize, I would say that, having regard to all aspects of the question, the answer is both yes and no. Yes, it looks as if it is possible for him to depart from the living God and apostatize; and no, he cannot do so, or to put it in a better way, he will not do so.

First, it *is* possible for the Christian to go back in this way. Paul in his epistles mourns over those of his own circle who had apparently apostatized from the faith. One such was Alexander. "Alexander the coppersmith did me much evil: the Lord reward him according to his works; of whom be thou ware also, for he hath greatly withstood our words" (2 Tim. 4:14,15). It is interesting to note that in the next verse Paul speaks of some believers who forsook him at his first appearing before Nero, so that no man stood with him. He does not say of them what he said of Alexander, the Lord reward them according to their works, but rather, "I pray God it may not be laid to their charge." They were weak believers who, to use a colloquialism, "chickened out" of their stand for Christ and for His servant because of fear. Alexander was quite other than this; he was a deliberate apostate, as another reference to him makes clear: "of whom [those who had made shipwreck of their faith] is Hymenaeus and Alexander; whom I have delivered unto Satan, that they may learn not to blaspheme" (1 Tim. 1:20). He refers to this Hymenaeus elsewhere, not only as an apostate, but a teacher of erroneous doctrine, doing much harm among the saints: "And their word will eat as doth a canker: of whom is Hymenaeus and Philetus; who concerning the truth have erred, saying that the resurrection is past already; and overthrow the faith of some" (2 Tim. 2:17,18).

There are more cases that could be quoted in the epistles, not only of Paul but also of Peter, John, and Jude. It will not do for us to try to dismiss the difficulty by saying that these were not professing Christians to begin with. Had they only been men of the world, outside the church, their state would not have been the subject of such deep concern and comment. It was the fact that they once confessed Christ that burdened the apostles so much. Yes, the early church had their share of disappointments and apostates, as we have today. Everyone charged in any degree with responsibility for the flock of God knows at least some cases of those who have not only drifted from God in the first place and then become hardened through the deceitfulness of sin, but have finally departed from the living God and repudiated their faith; and yet they seemed to show evidences of spiritual life at the beginning. There may not be many such, but there are enough of them to demonstrate that this is a solemn possibility for a professing Christian and that he needs to heed the earnest warnings of this great epistle.

Enduring to the End

Having loved his own which were in rhe world, he loved them unto the end.

Who shall also confirm you unto the end, that ye may be blameless in the day of our Lord Jesus Christ. God is faithful, by whom ye were called into the fellowship of his Son Jesus Christ our Lord.

And I pray God your whole spirit and soul and body be preserved blameless unto the coming of our Lord Jesus Christ. Faithful is he that calleth you, who also will do it.

— John 13:1; 1 Corinthians 1:8,9; 1 Thessalonians 5:23,24

9

Enduring to the End

WE HAVE SAID that the answer to the question Can a Christian apostatize? is both yes and no. We have considered the first part of that answer: yes, it seems he can. We come now to the other side of the coin, the much more encouraging side. It is not so much that it is impossible for him to do so, but, if he is a true child of God, he will not do so; God guarantees that he will persevere in holiness, and that right to the end, and thus be saved from getting anywhere near that end-of-the-road place. Paul was completely confident of this: "Being confident of this very thing," he wrote to the Philippians, "that he which hath begun a good work in you will perform it until the day of Jesus Christ" (1:6). Their salvation did not begin with themselves, neither will its continuance depend on themselves. It was God who took the initiative in seeking them out and finding them; and the same blessed One is going to continue taking the initiative with them all the way through. Left to themselves, they would certainly peter out in their Christian course and might even apostatize; but they are not going to be left to themselves. God, by whom they were called into the fellowship of His Son, is going to be faithful (1 Cor. 1:9). It is not that the saints have any residual power in themselves that makes them immune from falling. Faced as they are with a trinity of evil — the world their external foe, the flesh their internal foe, and the devil their infernal foe — they are prone right up to their dying day to wander, deviate, and go back. If they persevere in holiness, as they will, it will not be as a result of their own strength or determination, nor will they be able to claim any credit for it — God will be the doer of it. Spurgeon said, "The saints will persevere in holiness only because God will persevere in grace." That is the secret and that only. This means that not only does God get all the glory in their salvation, which is all of grace, but also in their perseverance to the end, which is also all of grace.

What we are considering here is what is called by theologians the final perseverance of the saints; and it is not the same as the eternal security of the believer. His eternal security, that is, the fact that he has eternal life and will never perish, is not based on any perseverance in holiness on his part, nor even on that which has been inwrought by the Holy Spirit, but solely on the value God sets on the blood of His Son on his behalf. The work of the Holy Spirit within us can never be regarded as a finished work; there will always be more He will need to deal with us about, always more that He will need to impart to us. It will at best be only a relative holiness, not an absolute one, which belongs to God alone. It can never, therefore, be his title to eternal security; there is no "solid rock" about it. In any case, after years of the Spirit's work within him, the believer will always have cause to take his place before God as a sinner. If, however, the work of the Spirit in us is never finished, there is another work that is — the finished work of Christ for us on the cross. That is enough for all the believer's sins; God has declared Himself eternally satisfied with it in that He raised Jesus our Lord from the dead (Rom. 4:25).

> If Jesus had not paid the debt,
> He ne'er had been at freedom set.

It is this that gives the believer his title to know himself eternally saved. This is the solid rock beneath his feet. To build on anything in himself is to build on sinking sand.

What we are considering in this chapter, however, is other than this. It is the perseverance of that saved one in holiness and that right to the end. Of course, the holiness in which he will persevere will be a gospel holiness, what we may call a repenting holiness, "holding the beginning of his confidence steadfast to the end," that is, confidence in grace, as has been previously explained. He is capable of nothing else. But that he shall so continue in this way is pledged by God Himself. Though he fall, he will rise again. He will not be permitted finally to depart from the living God and reach that end-of-the-road place. Rather, he will be presented faultless before the presence of God's glory with exceeding joy.

WHAT ARE THE PROCESSES?

We must now ask, By what processes does God's unchanging grace toward the believer insure his continuance to the end? for this does not happen "just like that," merely because God has willed it so. In answering that question, we must understand, first of all, that the one God is working on is a person in whom the flesh still dwells, although he is a believer and a new creature in Christ. This means that he is still capable of acting and reacting in a self-regarding way; he can still fall into sin; he can still grow spiritually cold and get away from God. And he is not merely capable of doing all this, but he actually does so on all too many occasions. In fact, the paradox is that the nearer he gets to God and the brighter the light shines, the more he sees places where this is indeed happening; darkness had blinded his eyes before. This, then, is the man God guarantees will persevere in holiness to the end; and the question we ask is, How?

First of all, when the Holy Spirit regenerated him, God put a new principle of life within him. Although the flesh is still there, the Holy Spirit is there too and also the new nature which He has created. This means the believer will not be happy when he falls into sin. If "the sow that was washed has returned to her wallowing in the mire" (Peter's metaphor in his second epistle), it is because she belongs there and is at home there. Not so the sheep; if that creature falls into the mire, he will be distressed and will not be content until he has extricated himself. Now the believer is said to be a new creature — "If any man be in Christ, he is a new creature" (2 Cor. 5:17); once a sow, now a sheep! Where before he was at home in his sins and largely unconcerned about them, if he now falls into any of them again, he is troubled in heart until he has turned back to the Lord in confession. This new principle of life which has been put within him, then, always tends him to return. This is something wholly due to the grace of God.

Then again, more important than anything else, once he gets away from God, the Holy Spirit works to bring him back. If it is true that "the flesh lusteth against the Spirit," it is also true that "the Spirit lusteth against the flesh" (Gal. 5:17). The Spirit does so by disturbing his peace, convicting him of sin, wrestling with his stubborn will, showing him the grace that awaits him at the Cross and revealing the many better things that are in Christ for him if he forsakes the ways of sin. So he is brought back to the Cross time and again.

> Perverse and foolish oft I strayed,
> And yet in love He sought me;
> And on His shoulder gently laid,
> And home rejoicing brought me.

Perseverance to the end is far more the perseverance of the Shepherd than that of the sheep.

Then further, as the believer repents of what the Holy Spirit shows him, the same Spirit works in him those qualities of holiness which he confesses he lacks. Under the new covenant God puts into him what He wants out of him — it is the believer's only hope of holiness, and grace will not fail him in his helplessness. As a result, he finds himself possessed of a love, a gentleness, a zeal, and an endurance which is not native to him.

More than that, the Lord Jesus knows how to manifest Himself to the believer, so that he finds himself so attracted to and excited by Him as to want to run after Him, as it is written in the Song of Solomon: "Draw me, we will run after thee" (1:4). The same thought of Jesus attracting and stimulating the believer is contained in another picture in the same book: "He standeth behind our wall, he looketh in at the windows, flourishing Himself through the lattice," and saying, "Rise up, my love, my fair one, and come away" (2:9,10). Yes, Jesus knows how to flourish Himself before the saddened believer cooped up, as he sometimes is, under the law and filled with self-recrimination. He bids him come away and dance again with Him on the mountains in the springtime of grace — and dance again he does.

Yet further, the Lord Jesus does not fail to come to him in his times of trouble and persecution, when the pressure on him to draw back is intense. He knows how to stimulate him to "endure as seeing him who is invisible," giving him sights of Himself as His heavenly High Priest, ever living to make intercession for him and to impart all the abundance of life and joy he needs. He shows him the faithfulness of God and the "recompence of the reward" that awaits those that suffer for Him. Nor does He fail to give him grace, if it should come to the ultimate alternative of going forward to imprisonment and martyrdom, "not accepting deliverance, that he might obtain a better resurrection" (Heb. 11:35).

These are some of the many processes by which God perseveres in grace toward us that we might endure to the end.

And persevere He must, for the material He has to work on is poor, as we are weak and vacillating. But "he shall not fail, nor be discouraged" (Isa. 42:4) till He has completed the work He began. So it is that Toplady sings with confidence,

> And I to the end shall endure,
> As sure as the earnest is given;
> More happy, but not more secure,
> When glorified with Him in heaven.

In that one stanza we have the doctrines of the final perseverance of the saints and the eternal security of the believer perfectly joined together as twins — not quite "identical twins," but twins nevertheless.

See, then, the saint's complete dependence on the grace of God continuing toward him to the end. David said of the position he was in as Saul pursued him, "There is but a step between me and death." The saint on his part says, "There is nothing but Christ between me and death." But for Him, he could slip away, become hardened, and finally apostatize. Between even the most mature Christian and that awesome end there is nothing but Christ. Does that trouble you and make you feel insecure? "After being a Christian all these years," you might say, "surely there is some residual holiness in me that would prohibit me from going to such lengths!" There is no such thing as residual holiness, either native to us or acquired by us, and if there were, it would offer us no safeguard. There is only Christ between us and death — but is He not enough? Will He ever fail in His perseverance toward us? Could there be a greater safeguard against "drawing back to perdition" than just Himself?

> And there between us stands the cross,
> Two arms outstretched to save,
> Like a watchman set to guard the way
> From that eternal grave.

PROVED A COUNTERFEIT

We come now to the next important question: What are we to make of the once-professing Christian who never returns to the Lord, but continues on his outward course and ultimately reaches that end-of-the-road place of finally repudiating his faith? This simply proves him never to have been a true child of God and all along to have been a counterfeit. Though he may not have appeared so at the time, the event has proved it. This is a truth taught in Scripture, and as I have looked into it, I am surprised to find how much there is of it.

A basic passage on this point is 2 Corinthians 13:5, where Paul says, "Examine yourselves, whether ye be in the faith; prove your own selves. Know ye not your own selves, how that Jesus Christ is in you, except ye be reprobates?" In this verse, the Greek word translated "prove" is *dokimazete*, and the word for "reprobate" is simply the negative *adokimos* (the prefix *a* turning it into a negative). The secular use of these words would be with regard to the testing of metals, as when an assayer tests silver and gold to see if they are the substance and of the quality they purport to be. The word *reprobate*, then, conveys the picture of a metal that has failed the test and been found a counterfeit, and thus must be rejected. The word *disapproved* might be another translation that could help us, but for the Elizabethan readers of the King James Version there was no difficulty in understanding the word *reprobate* as referring to a metal that had been proved worthless. Indeed, it is used with just this connotation in Jeremiah 6:30: "Reprobate silver shall men call them." What Paul is saying in this verse, then, is that the distinguishing fact about a true Christian is that Jesus Christ is in him, unless on test he is found to be a counterfeit. And the test as to whether a professed believer is true or false is whether he continues in the faith to the end. If he does not do so, but ends rather in open apostasy, then it is clear he was only a counterfeit all along. This does not necessarily mean that he was deliberately deceiving others during that time and putting on an act; more likely he was just self-deceived; but the event has proved the truth. Not that everyone who is a counterfeit must of necessity end as an apostate. Many who have never known the new birth have continued making a religious profession to the end, but will be rejected as reprobate nonetheless. What it does mean is that those who do end in an apostate condition are clearly proved by that fact to have been counterfeit, for grace guarantees the perseverance of the true saint to the end.

These are exactly the sort of people the apostle John refers to with such sadness in his first epistle, 2:19. "They went out from us, but they were not of us; for if they had been of us, they would no doubt have continued with us; but they went out, that they might be made manifest they were not all of us." These people had appeared to be true believers and had been in fellowship with the church on the basis that they were. But the fact that they "went out" proved to John that "they were not of us" and had never truly been so. Moreover, inasmuch as the subject of the previous verse is Antichrist and that "even now are there many antichrists," it would suggest that those who had "gone out" had done so to become, not merely backsliders, but active opponents of the very message and people they had once espoused.

Another reference I would turn you to is John 8:31 where

our Lord says to the Jews who believed on Him: "If ye continue in my word, then are ye *my disciples indeed,*" that is, real disciples, not counterfeit ones. The proof that they were genuine would be that they would continue in His Word; if they did not so continue, then they were not the real thing at all. For an illustration, we can go back to Peter's picture of the sow that was washed returning to her wallowing in the mire. If she does so and is at home there, it shows that she was still only a sow that had been washed. It might have seemed like a sheep to some, but it was only a sow, after all. It had, therefore, been no part of that flock of sheep of which Jesus is the Shepherd.

Yet another passage is 2 Timothy 2:19: "Nevertheless the foundation of God standeth sure, having this seal, The Lord knoweth them that are his. And, Let everyone that nameth the name of Christ depart from iniquity." If, however, a professed Christian does not depart from iniquity, but rather departs from the Lord, and that in the decisive way we have indicated, then we can only assume he is not one of "them that are his."

If you are familiar with the five pregnant chapters of John's first epistle, you will know that this is the disturbing logic that he relentlessly pursues all the way through. He refuses to recognize as a child of God at all those who are not manifesting the fruits of that relationship, but are living in sin and darkness, and that in spite of what they may profess. To quote but two verses: "He that saith he is in the light, and hateth his brother, is in darkness even until now" (2:9) and "In this the children of God are manifest, and the children of the devil: whosoever doeth not righteousness is not of God, neither he that loveth not his brother" (3:10). I do not quote more verses, for there are so many; in any case, it is far more an emphasis that runs all the way through, in which John challenges an inconsistent profession. Note, for instance, the recurrence of the phrase "if we say" or "he that saith" in the first two chapters. This teaching certainly has bearing on what we are considering — the solemn possibility of a professed Christian being only a counterfeit.

Whereas this does not for a moment touch the security of those whose Shepherd Jesus is, it does constitute a call to us to examine ourselves as to whether we have truly become one of His sheep by new birth, and are not counterfeit. This is just what Paul tells us to do in the verse already quoted: "Examine yourselves whether ye be in the faith," implying that we can be "coasting along" thinking all is well with us, when in reality we are not in the faith at all. It might be found that ours is not a first-hand faith but a second-hand one, derived from parents or Christian friends. We might discover that we have never seen ourselves as total sinners, subject to the judgment of God, with no hope but in the Cross of Jesus. It could be that there have always been reservations in our surrender to God, issues over which we have not been willing to repent, and citadels we have not allowed Him to capture. If on examination of yourself, you find this to be so, there need be no cause for despair: "If any man sin, we have an advocate with the Father, Jesus Christ the righteous" (1 John 2:1). You can do business with God at the Cross, this time in reality, and receive what grace has for you. In this way you will "make your calling and election sure" (2 Peter 1:10).

A THREEFOLD ASSURANCE

It might be asked how one can be sure that one is born of God. We can trace in the Scriptures a threefold ground of assurance of salvation for the believer. The first is external, that is, the promises of God that cannot be broken, assuring the believer that he has eternal life and will not perish: "He that heareth my word, and believeth on him that sent me, hath everlasting life, and shall not come into condemnation; but is passed from death unto life" (John 5:24). There are many other such promises. The believer casts his anchor onto something outside of himself that cannot be shaken, the faithfulness of God, and ceases to judge his salvation by the state of his feelings.

The second ground of assurance is internal, the inner witness of the Holy Spirit that he is a child of God: "The Spirit himself beareth witness with our spirit, that we are children of

God" (Rom. 8:16). This is, of course, more subjective than the first, and by itself would not be enough to assure the believer when Satan attacks him with doubts. It is nonetheless his privilege to have the Holy Spirit constantly whispering in his heart that God is his Father and he His child, and when he has that witness, all hell cannot make him believe otherwise — he just knows!

The third is evidential, that is, the appearance in his life and experience of clear evidence that he is not what he once was and that he is born of God. If John in his first epistle continually exposes an inconsistent profession, he comforts us by pointing to various evidences that we have passed from death to life, that we might assure our hearts before God. Here we have the more frequent recurrence of another phrase, "hereby we know," or words like those, in the following verses: 2:3; 2:5; 3:14; 3:19; 3:24; 4:13; 5:13; 5:19. Look them up. So it is that we have in John's epistle not only "if we say" but, more important, "hereby we know." Indeed, the whole of the little epistle is written that "ye may know that ye have eternal life" (5:13). As we browse over these references, we get the message that it is not merely we who want the blessed assurance, but, much more, He who wants us to have it.

WILL I ENDURE TO THE END?

Even so, the believer may sometimes tremble and in the face of the solemn warnings of this Hebrew epistle, fear lest he will not continue to the end, lest he might one day depart from the living God and at last be proved a counterfeit. These lines, quoted in one of Spurgeon's sermons, sum up how the Christian may feel sometimes:

> When any turn from Zion's way,
>   (Alas what numbers do),
> Methinks, I hear my Saviour say,
>   "Wilt thou forsake Me too?"
>
> Ah, Lord, with such a heart as mine,
>   Unless Thou hold me fast,
> I feel I must, I shall, decline
>   And prove like them at last.

Is that how you feel? May I say that you are in a healthy state, indeed, in a safe place, if you do. The man who truly says all that about himself, adding "unless Thou hold me fast," is the one man who is not going to decline and "prove like them at last." God *is* going to hold him fast. His acknowledgment of weakness makes him a candidate for the grace of God as nothing else does. The trouble with the others was that they never saw this deep perversity in them, nor their dependence on the persevering grace of God toward them. If you are distrustful of yourself, if you know all too well what you are capable of but are casting yourself on Jesus, you need not fear; yours is exactly the raw material in which He delights to work; He *will* not let you go; He *will* cause you to walk in His statutes; He *will* work "in you that which is well-pleasing in His sight through Jesus Christ" (13:21) and you *will* endure to the end. Listen to the promise of grace that should settle every doubt on this score: "Who shall confirm you *unto the end,* that ye may be blameless in the day of our Lord Jesus Christ" (1 Cor. 1:8). For how much of the way will He continue to confirm and strengthen you? *To the end!* And what is His purpose in so doing? "That ye may be blameless in the day of our Lord Jesus Christ" — that ye be shown to be no apostate, no reprobate, nor anywhere near it. Dear trembling one who believes in Jesus, hear the words of promise that He Himself said: "This is the Father's will which hath sent me, that of all which He hath given me I should lose nothing, but should raise it up again at the last day" (John 6:39).

WHY THE WARNING?

Before we leave this chapter, one further question must be answered. It might be asked, If our enduring to the end is so sure, guaranteed by the faithfulness of God Himself, why are we subject to the strong warnings and exhortations of the Epistle to the Hebrews, as if it is something we have to do, as if the issue was in doubt?

Here we come to yet another paradox of divine truth; we are simply facing the old dichotomy between divine sovereignty and human responsibility. Both of these are true. God purposes, predestinates, calls, justifies, and glorifies whom He will; but man is bidden to come and it is his responsibility to choose whether or not he does — life or death depend upon it for him. It is quite impossible for finite minds like ours to work out a harmonization between these two apparently opposite truths, but they are both presented in Scripture with a perfect and right balance.

Now this dichotomy between God's purposing and man's choosing is usually thought of as relating to our initial salvation. But it applies equally to our continuing to the end after we are saved. As in conversion, man has the responsibility to respond and to cooperate with God. His responsibility is not to originate — that God is doing — but to cooperate. The cooperation required is not for him to struggle to do his best and make promises, but to respond to the initiatives of grace. It is for him to repent when the Spirit says, "Repent"; it is to judge himself when the Spirit shows him his sin; it is to obey and do the thing God calls him to, counting on Him to put into him what he knows is not there naturally. Above all, it means holding the beginning of his confidence in grace steadfast to the end (3:14), as has already been explained.

It was only by this grace that Paul could say as he neared his end: "I have fought a good fight, I have finished my course, I have kept the faith" (2 Tim. 4:7) — that is, I have endured to the end without apostatizing from the faith. Paul did not take it as a matter of course that he had done so. It was a marvelous thing for which he could only thank God who had persevered in grace with him all the way through. Then he goes on to say, "Henceforth there is laid up for me a crown of righteousness, which the Lord, the righteous judge, shall give me at that day." This crown is, of course, not salvation; he has already been in the enjoyment of that for the long years of his Christian course; it is, rather, the reward of Jesus for His faithful warrior. And inasmuch as the faithfulness for which he is being rewarded was not his work but the Lord's work in him, I think I know what he will do with that crown; he will not put it on his own head, but lay it at the feet of the One who has done it all, and doubtless sing something like this:

> This, my song through endless ages,
> Jesus led me all the way.

So shall we certainly endure right to the end; so shall we keep our armor bright and not despair till we are presented blameless before the Father. Jude was celebrating this grace of God when he uttered his glorious doxology:

> Now unto him that is able to keep you from falling and to present you faultless before the presence of his glory with exceeding joy, to the only wise God our Saviour, be glory and majesty, dominion and power both now and ever. Amen.

We have good cause therefore, to sing,

> Through many dangers, toils, and snares,
> I have already come;
> 'Tis grace that brought me safe thus far,
> And grace will lead me home.

Is the Apostate
Irrecoverable?

10

Is the Apostate Irrecoverable?

NOW WE COME to the question as to whether the state of apostasy of which we have spoken is irrecoverable.

Before considering this matter, it will be well for us to recapitulate some of the ground covered in the last two chapters. We have been faced with a series of balanced truths, which seem almost like contradictions. First, we have seen that it is sadly possible for a professing Christian to repudiate his faith and apostatize; then, that the one truly born of God would be safely kept from ever doing so; then, that if deliberate apostasy does take place in a life, it demonstrates that the person concerned never was truly born of God, that he was only a counterfeit Christian, a reprobate, no matter how like the real thing he might have appeared at one time.

There is, however, in the last case, no lack of mercy available, for grace knows nothing of a mysterious "point of no return" which we might possibly pass over. Even the one who has indeed apostatized may always begin again; the door of mercy is as open to him as it ever was. It is only the person who persistently refuses and ends his days in this condition of apostasy who is ultimately rejected.

This brings us, then, to the question of this chapter: Is apostasy irrecoverable? The answer is, of course, no. As long as the words of the old hymn represent an eternal truth,

> Dear dying Lamb, Thy precious blood
> Shall never lose its power,
> Till all the ransomed Church of God
> Be saved to sin no more,

the way back to God and to peace is always open, even for the most blatant apostate. A man dies in his sins only while he is in his sins. Grace would not be grace if one category of sinner was excluded. Jesus anticipated even the sin of the apostate in His body on the tree. He must return and repent, of course, and a heart long hardened might find that difficult, but that the door of salvation is still open to him there can be no doubt. Moreover, we must not make too much of the text "My spirit shall not always strive with man" (Gen. 6:3); who can estimate the long-suffering of God, or gauge the point at which His Spirit ceases to strive with a person? It is true that Paul had formally to exclude the two apostates, Hymenaeus and Alexander, from the fellowship of the church: "whom I have delivered unto Satan, that they might learn not to blaspheme" (1 Tim. 1:20). But there was always the possibility in his mind that they might learn something in that experience and be recovered. Always "there is hope of a tree if it be cut down that it will sprout again" (Job 14:7).

We do not take too seriously, then, the defiant statements of the apostate. They may be final as far as he is concerned, but not necessarily as far as God is concerned. The end of the story is not yet, not until he draws his final breath. We know what the Holy Spirit can do and that

> Ah, grace, it is Thy boast to come
> Into unlikeliest hearts.

I emphasize that apostasy is not irrecoverable, because there are at least three passages in this epistle which at first sight seem to suggest the opposite, that there is in fact a departing from the living God from which recovery is impossible. These passages have caused much distress to some people and usually they have been the very persons who had no cause to apply these passages against themselves. Their gloomy interpretations were based on a misunderstanding of their true meaning. Therefore, for the relief of souls, if for no other reason, we must proceed to examine these passages.

ESAU FOUND NO PLACE OF REPENTANCE

First let us turn to Hebrews 12:15-17:

> Looking diligently lest . . . there be any fornicator, or profane person, as Esau, who for one morsel of meat sold his birthright. For ye know how that afterward, when he would have inherited the blessing, he was rejected: for he found no place of repentance, though he sought it carefully with tears.

The Revised Standard Version only emphasizes the apparently cruel situation in which Esau appears to have found himself, by translating it: "He was rejected, because he had no chance to repent, though he sought it with tears."

At first sight, these verses do not seem exactly encouraging to other sinners who want to find peace. It was this verse that Satan used to the distress of John Bunyan, who thought for some two years he had committed a sin for which there was no forgiveness. Satan pointed him to the verse and said in effect, "Seek the place of repentance as earnestly as you will and with as many tears as Esau did — you will never find it!"

The true explanation of this verse is very simple and, strangely, very sweet. To repent simply means to change your mind; and in the story, when the blind Isaac discovered he had given the final blessing to Jacob rather than to Esau, he refused to change his mind. He said to Esau, "Where is he that hath taken venison, and brought it me, and I have eaten of all before thou camest, and have blessed him? *yea, and he shall be blessed*" (Gen. 27:33). Isaac saw in that moment that he had been wrong to be partial to Esau to the detriment of Jacob, that in choosing Esau he had chosen the man God had not chosen, and that God had overruled even Jacob's duplicity to have His will done. Therefore Isaac refused to change his mind, though Esau begged him with many tears to do so.

This passage, then, has nothing to do with a man desperately wanting the opportunity of repentance but not finding it. What a cruel interpretation, one that only the devil would try to apply to us!

It does, however, have an application to us, though of a different sort. It pictures the fact that God will not change His mind with regard to the terms on which He will bless men. The birthright which Esau sold for a plate of soup was something spiritual, the right of the eldest to be the family priest and to offer the sacrifice; moreover, it was the privilege of the eldest to know that from his line Messiah would one day come. That was a birthright that made little appeal to a secular man like Esau and one which he felt he could well do without. That which would satisfy his physical hunger was much more important to him, and he sold it for "one morsel of meat." The father's last blessing, however, he was now eager to have, for it meant earthly riches. The one who received it would become the heir and have bestowed on him the major portion of the family goods. He might be ready to sell his birthright cheap, but he had no intention of missing the blessing. But God saw to it that if he despised his birthright, he should forfeit the blessing. And nothing that Esau said could make either God or Isaac change their minds — no birthright, then no blessing.

The application to us is this. God has given a birthright to every child of Adam. As a member of the race for which God gave His Son, it is his birthright to know that Son as his personal Savior, to possess eternal life, to walk with Him all his days on earth and one day to stand with Him in glory. But God has decreed that, if a man despises his birthright and sells it for the things of the world, he will forfeit the blessings that are associated with it — the blessing of a peaceful heart, a happy home, a loving providence, innumerable compensations for the sometime sadness of earthly life, and one day an eternity in heaven. But things turn out the very opposite of that for the sinner, and, when realizing what he has lost, he utters the "exceeding great and bitter cry" that Esau did, it will be impossible to get God to repent, that is, change His mind. If a man has despised his birthright, then he shall forfeit the blessing; if a man will not have Christ, then he cannot have those infinitely desirable things, which even the sinner admits to be desirable, that go with Him.

But while it is impossible to get God to change His mind, the sinner can change his mind, the sinner can repent, while he has breath. Jesus is all the time offering him his birthright back again; and when a man consents to have it back, Jesus makes good all the losses he has suffered.

That is the application we can make of this Scripture, a warning one, but a loving one. The application that would simply torture the saints is not of God. The devil is the accuser of the brethren, but the Holy Spirit is the encourager of them.

No More Sacrifice for Sins

Another passage we must turn to is Hebrews 10:26,27.

> For if we sin wilfully after that we have received the knowledge of the truth, there remaineth no more sacrifice for sins, but a certain fearful looking for of judgment and fiery indignation, which shall devour the adversaries.

This is stark indeed and at first sight seems to be a contradiction of all the mighty encouragements of the rest of the epistle. When we look closer, we find this is not so at all.

I must refer you back to the special danger these professed Hebrew Christians were in. They had seen that Christ's offering of Himself on the cross was the final offering that did away with all others, the substance that made all other sacrifices but shadows. As a result of this sacrifice, God was willing to remember their sins and iniquities no more. Now if these Hebrews really confessed their faith in this one Offering and forsook the many shadow-offerings of Judaism, they would doubtless involve themselves in much more opposition and suffering than they had experienced before. Their peril was that they might in such a situation want to retreat from the confession of their faith to the old sacrifices of the earthly altar and find refuge there. Paul says here in effect, "You cannot go back there, for you know there is nothing to go back to. There remains no more sacrifice for sin of the old order, for they have all been robbed of significance by the work of Christ. If you sin now, you sin with your eyes open, knowing that if you do not go to the Cross, there is nothing for you but a certain looking for judgment and fiery indignation." The phrase "if we sin wilfully after we have received the knowledge of the truth" simply means committing known sin in the light of known truth, in which case it is either Calvary's Cross or judgment.

Once again, this is no application to the saint, in the sense that if he has sinned there is no further hope of recovery and no sacrifice for sin. The only application that could be made today (and it is a powerful one) is to the case of one whose trust, for instance, has always been in the church and her sacraments. But he has heard the gospel and understands that there is no peace for the sinner except in the Cross of Christ. He hesitates, fearing to go forth to the Cross, lest it should mean the censure, not only of the world, but of his coreligionists. He feels after all that it would be safer to remain where he was before, trusting in the ceremonies of the church, telling himself their very antiquity must give them some validity. Such a person must be told what Paul told the Hebrews, that he cannot, now that he has received the knowledge of the gospel, go back to trusting in them because they provide no sacrifice for sin. Having heard what he has, it is either Christ Himself, with nothing added to Him, or judgment.

This is a purely hypothetical case I picture, and I do not intend for a moment to denigrate the sacraments of the church, *except as objects of trust. That* they must never be; there is no healing efficacy in them, but only in the Cross and the heavenly high priesthood of Christ Himself.

Impossible to Renew Them to Repentance

The third passage to which we must turn is Hebrews 6:4-8:

For it is impossible for those who were once enlightened, and have tasted of the heavenly gift, and were made partakers of the Holy Ghost, and have tasted the good Word of God, and the powers of the world to come, if they shall fall away, to renew them again to repentance; seeing they crucify to themselves the Son of God afresh, and put him to an open shame. For the earth which drinketh in the rain which cometh upon it, and bringeth forth herbs meet for them by whom it is dressed, receiveth blessing from God: but that which beareth thorns and briars is rejected, and is nigh unto cursing; whose end is to be burned.

Here, too, is a passage which has caused distress to some, for in the light of it they have told themselves that, because they have fallen away, it is impossible for them to be renewed to repentance, and therefore there is no hope for them. In order to remove an apparent teaching that the true saints can lose their salvation and be unable to recover it, it has been customary to teach that the people referred to here were Christians only in name, that although they had gone along with others and been much influenced by the gospel, they lacked the essential life of the new birth. It is said, therefore, that there is no question here of it being impossible to renew a true saint to repentance, but only a nominal Christian.

However, a careful examination of the four descriptive phrases makes it very difficult to believe that they are not describing people who have been born anew. In any case, this explanation, while it removes one difficulty, creates another. Why should it be impossible to renew to repentance a nominal Christian who falls away from his profession? This explanation may be of comfort to the true saint, but it is not much of a gospel for the other fellow. In pastoral work, all of us would tell such an one he can begin again and allow the Lord to do a thorough work in his heart this time. It is true that the apostate may look like a believer for much of his course and that in the end it may be proved he was never a believer at all. But it is only the end that proves that. We are not right to assume that the description here is of apostates-in-the-making.

This has been a difficult verse to me as to many others. As I could not conceive of the believer's security in Christ being challenged by the verse as it stood, I was much inclined to accept the customary view in spite of its deficiencies and without being fully satisfied with it. It was only after I had spent many years in evangelistic work that an old minister in the Church of England gave me a book to read on this passage. In this book I found an exposition that really satisfied me and did not merely explain away the problem, but gave a positive message in keeping with the whole epistle. I have never been able to trace that book since then nor recall the author, and the one who allowed me to read it has long since passed away, but I took full notes and I share the exposition in the hope that it will be as helpful to you as it has been to me.

NOT LAYING FOUNDATIONS TWICE OVER

It is important to note that these verses are part of the whole section from verses 1 to 8, a section which begins with the call for us to go on to perfection, or full growth, "not laying again the foundation of repentance from dead works and of faith toward God." I think we can entitle the theme of this passage "Not laying foundations twice over." What Paul says on this theme can be summarized under three heads.

First, *do not lay foundations twice over.* We are not to lay again the foundation of the initial repentance and faith and new birth every time there has been failure or lapsing in the Christian life, as if the foundation had not already been laid and as if it did not abide. Paul says in another place, "Other foundation can no man lay than that is laid, which is Jesus Christ" (1 Cor. 3:11). Foundations are to be built on, not to be continually relaid. The lapsed believer does not need to be led back to a conversion experience, but on to a place of full growth, or maturity, where Jesus, his heavenly Melchizedek, takes care of his current failures and imparts the fullness of His life to him. The passage is not dealing with the possibility of losing one's salvation, but rather with pastoral methods; whether one leads the believer, who has fallen away, back to lay his original foundation again, or on into the fullness of Christ. To do the former is to produce Christians who do not grow up and who can never take anything more than the most elementary truths. To do the latter is to enable them to judge themselves with regard to their failure where they are and to go on to life with Jesus in the Holiest.

Second, *it is impossible to lay foundations twice over.* It is an impossibility in the nature of the case; a foundation is something that cannot be continually laid again. And the people described here are those who already have the foundation. They are described as those "who were once enlightened, and have tasted of the heavenly gift, and were made partakers of the Holy Ghost and have tasted the good word of God, and the powers of the world to come." What is this but a declaration that they had the foundation of the new birth? It is impossible to lay that foundation again, simply because it is already there. What has given this verse a wrong twist is the undue prominence the translators have given to the phrase "if they shall fall away." The people referred to in the verse are described by a number of past participles in the Greek — having been enlightened, having tasted the heavenly gift, having been partakers of the Holy Spirit and so on. "Having fallen away" is simply one of these past participles. It is not "if they shall fall away," but just a past participle like the others and should be given no more prominence than they. But the translators in almost every version have been so fascinated by the difficult doctrine they thought they saw in the verse that they walked right into the problem and gave the phrase such a prominence as to make it look as if the main topic is the matter of a falling away from which there is no recovery, which is not the topic at all. The verse should simply make the point that it is impossible to renew to repentance those who had already been enlightened and been made partakers of the Holy Spirit and thus had the foundation of repentance already. The fact that these people had fallen away is almost, one might say, incidental, certainly no more prominent than the other four things that are said about them. Of course, they had indeed fallen away, otherwise there would be no question of their needing to be renewed, but that is not the main point of the verse.

Then, too, another source of misunderstanding has been the fact that most of us have read into the words "if they shall fall away" a more awesome meaning than the Greek word warrants. "Falling away" in the accepted sense is too strong for the Greek word, *parapipto;* "having side-stepped" would be a more helpful expression. There is no question here of these people having apostatized. The Revised Version has without any warrant blithely translated it "if they then commit apostasy. . . ." The Greek word for apostasy does not appear here at all. It is not even as strong a word as the expression "depart from the living God" in chapter 3, but a much weaker word, meaning literally, to fall sideways, that is, to side-step or side-slip. This is something that can happen all too easily in a believer's life. There is no excusing it, of course; it can be grievous and must be judged as sin, but there is no implication in it that one is apostatizing. The notes I have of what our unknown author wrote illumine this point helpfully: "David in 2 Samuel 11 'sideslipped' terribly and put his God to an open shame, but he was not ungodly, he did not need renewing as to his direction." It is impossible, then, to lay again a foundation that is already there; we need to be led on, not continually back.

Thirdly, you *need not lay these foundations twice over.* Here we are looking at verse 8, which speaks of the unfruitful ground: "But that which beareth thorns and briars is rejected and is nigh unto cursing; whose end is to be burned." To quote from my notes again: "God's chastening judgment will deal with the unfruitful believer, and his work shall be burned, though he himself will be saved, 'yet so as by fire' (1 Cor. 3:15). Therefore there is no need for him to go back to the foundation of initial repentance, but rather he is to count his backslidden works as doomed to be burned and go on to perfection, full growth, leaving what chastening may be involved in the hands of his heavenly Father as David did."

Enough has been said, then, to show that the state of the apostate is not an irrecoverable one and that the three passages we have dealt with do not in fact teach that it is. The door of mercy still stands open for the most vehement Christ-rejector, whether he be one who has made a profession, or not. He may yet repent and turn to Christ, confident that he will be received.

WHAT IF HE NEVER REPENTS?

We now come to the question, What if he never does repent? and, of course, it is only too possible that he may not. God on His part will not coerce him. He will through the ambassadors of His Son "persuade men" and even "beseech them" (2 Cor. 5:11,20), but He will not violate the free will He Himself has conferred upon them. And they on their part can always use that free will against the One who has given it them. C. S. Lewis writes in his chapter on "Hell" in *The Problem of Pain:* "It has been admitted all through that man has free will and that all gifts to him are therefore two-edged. From these premises it follows directly that the Divine labour to redeem the world cannot be certain of succeeding as regards every individual soul. Some will not be redeemed."

What then? There is nothing for them "but a certain looking for of judgment and fiery indignation which shall devour the adversaries" (10:27). Whereas in God's vocabulary the opposite to sin is grace, the alternative to grace for the one who refuses it, is judgment. And this judgment is described in this epistle in the most solemn terms: "It is a fearful thing to fall into the hands of the living God" (10:31) and "Our God is a consuming fire" (12:29). One further verse in another part of the Scriptures may be quoted as representative of many:

> The Lord Jesus shall be revealed from heaven with his mighty angels, in flaming fire taking vengeance on them that know not God, and that obey not the gospel of our Lord Jesus Christ: who shall be punished with everlasting destruction from the presence of the Lord, and from the glory of his power (2 Thess. 1:7-9).

The word *fire* is obviously used in a metaphorical sense; but if the metaphor is fire, what must the reality be? On any showing, the fate of the Christ-rejector is a terrible one indeed. There is no doctrine that most of us would be more ready to expunge from Christianity, if it were in our power. But it has the full support of Scripture, especially of our Lord's words.

A PROBLEM

There is, however, a problem here. To quote C. S. Lewis again: "So much mercy, yet still there is hell." It must be remembered, however, that the judgment of the sinner is introduced only after the fullest mercy for him has been revealed and as the only possible alternative if that mercy is spurned. Indeed, this epistle makes clear an even more awesome fact, that under the gospel, where the blessings are

infinitely greater than under the law of Moses, the penalties for
rejecting it are greater too.

> For if the word spoken by angels was steadfast, and every trans-
> gression and disobedience received a just recompence of reward;
> how shall we escape, if we neglect so great salvation; which at the
> first began to be spoken by the Lord and was confirmed unto us by
> them that heard him (2:2,3).

And again:

> He that despised Moses' law died without mercy under two or three
> witnesses; of how much sorer punishment, suppose ye shall he be
> thought worthy, who hath trodden under foot the Son of God, and
> hath counted the blood of the covenant, wherewith he was sanc-
> tified, an unholy thing, and hath done despite unto the Spirit of
> grace? (10:28,29).

And again:

> For if they escaped not, who refused him that spake on earth, much
> more shall not we escape, if we turn away from him that speaketh
> from heaven (12:25).

You see, under the law, if a person was responsive at all, it was
the junior pleading with the Senior; but under grace, it is the
Senior, if you please, pleading with the junior. Under law it
was man at God's feet; under grace it is the Son of God at man's
feet, pleading with him; Jesus took that place when He washed
the disciples' feet, and He made Himself vulnerable in so
doing. This means that under the gospel man can commit a far
greater sin than he could under law — he can trample under his
feet the One who is kneeling there. And because he can
commit this far greater sin, the punishment is far greater too.
The epistle tells us twice that for those who do so, there is no
escape (2:3; 12:25).

A Further Offer of Mercy

And yet, even in revealing the terrible end of the Christ-
rejector, God is only making a further offer of mercy. Indeed,
that is His only reason for making any announcements of
coming judgment at all. It might be asked, If God had decided
that the impenitent shall be judged and cast into hell, why does
He not just do it, without talking so much about it beforehand?

The same might be asked of the many prophecies of doom that Jeremiah had to speak against Israel and Judah, how they were to be overthrown and taken into captivity. If that is what their sin deserved, why did God not simply do it without giving these incessant prophecies about it through Jeremiah? The same question might also be asked about Jonah's prophecy against Nineveh. If God had decided that Nineveh's sins merited their destruction, why did He not accomplish it immediately, without sending Jonah to tell the Ninevites that it was going to happen, and strangely, not until after six weeks' time?

Obviously, it is *because the message of judgment is always the offer of mercy.* This is a beautiful and tender theme all through Scripture. Jeremiah was told on more than one occasion why God had given him these many prophecies against Israel:

It may be that the house of Judah will hear all the evil which I purpose to do unto them; that they may return every man from his evil way; that I may forgive their iniquity and their sin (36:3).

There are two further places in Jeremiah where we have the same plaintive, "It may be . . . " (26:3; 36:7). It was because God was "longsuffering . . . not willing that any should perish, but that all should come to repentance" (2 Peter 3:9).

This was the reason why God commanded Jonah to tell the Ninevites: "Yet forty days, and Nineveh shall be destroyed" (Jonah 3:4). It was really an offer of mercy and He gave them nearly six weeks in which to repent of their sins so that He might forgive them and not have to do what otherwise was inevitable. And that is exactly what happened:

So the people of Nineveh believed God, and proclaimed a fast, and put on sackcloth from the greatest of them even to the least of them (3:5).

This was not merely an outward sign of mourning, for the king commanded them:

Let man and beast be covered with sackcloth and cry mightily unto God: yea, let them turn everyone from his evil way, and from the violence that is in their hands (3:8).

There was in their prayer only an elementary faith that God might be gracious:

> Who can tell if God will turn and repent, and turn away from his fierce anger, that we perish not? (3:9).

Uncertain as that faith in His mercy was — just a who-can-tell — it was enough for God:

> And God saw their works that they turned from their evil way; and God repented of the evil, that he said he would do unto them; and he did it not (3:10).

And God was delighted — a truly scriptural phrase, by the way, for "he delighteth in mercy" (Mic. 7:18)! The only one who was not delighted was Jonah, who thought that God was too soft (4:2) — an unpleasant anticipation of the elder son criticizing the father for his mercy to the prodigal!

The same is true of these judgment passages in the epistle we are considering. They are but further offers of mercy to the Christ-rejector and further inducements for him to repent before it is too late. "It may be they will hear . . . that they may return . . . that I may forgive. . . ." What a lovable God, then, is here presented, even in His messages of judgment!

If this be the purpose of the message of death, judgment, and hell, the preacher today need have no inhibitions at all in preaching it. It is only a demonstration of God's love and of the preacher's own love for sinners. Indeed, if he is not doing so, it may be questioned whether he really loves the people to whom God has sent him. The one who preaches about hell does so only because he is so deeply concerned that men should not go there.

And as for any reader of these lines who is undecided in his mind and unsure as to whether he is ready for eternity, I would urge him, by what Paul rightly called "the terror of the Lord," to get right with God and do it now. Answer the question "Where will you spend eternity?" as E. A. Hoffman bids you answer it:

> Where will you spend eternity?
> This question comes to you and me!
> Tell me, what shall your answer be —
> Where will you spend eternity?

Many are choosing Christ today,
Turning from all their sins away;
Heaven shall their happy portion be:
Where will you spend eternity?

Leaving the straight and narrow way,
Going the downward road today,
Sad will the final ending be —
Lost through a long eternity?

Repent, believe this very hour,
Trust in the Saviour's grace and power;
Then shall your joyous answer be,
Saved through a long eternity.

The Race Set Before Us

Faith is the assurance of things hoped for, the conviction of things not seen . . .

> By faith Abel. . . . By faith Enoch. . . . By faith Noah. . . . By faith Abraham. . . . Through faith also Sarah. . . . By faith Isaac. . . . By faith Jacob. . . . By faith Moses. . . . By faith the harlot Rahab. . . . And what shall I more say? for the time would fail me to tell of Gideon, and of Barak, and of Samson, and of Jephthah; of David also, and Samuel, and of the prophets: who through faith subdued kingdoms, wrought righteousness, obtained promises, stopped the mouths of lions . . . and others were tortured, not accepting deliverance; that they might receive a better resurrection. . . .

Wherefore seeing we also are compassed about with so great a cloud of witnesses, let us lay aside every weight, and the sin which doth so easily beset us, and let us run with patience the race that is set before us, looking unto Jesus the author and finisher of our faith; who for the joy that was set before him endured the cross, despising the shame, and is set down at the right hand of the throne of God. For consider him that endured such contradiction of sinners against himself, lest ye be wearied and faint in your minds.

— Hebrews 11:1–12:3

11

The Race Set Before Us

THERE ARE THREE things "set before us" in the epistle. First, there is *"the hope set before us"* (6:18). This is the sinner's hope which we are to lay hold of when we flee to Jesus for refuge. Let us quote word for word this great verse: " . . . that by two immutable things, in which it was impossible for God to lie, we might have a strong consolation, who have fled for refuge to lay hold upon the hope set before us." Obviously, this is an allusion to the Old Testament provision of the six cities of refuge in Israel, to which a man who had killed another unawares and unwittingly might flee for refuge. The hope set before him, on which he was to lay hold, was the promise that, once inside, he would be safe from the avenger of blood, the next of kin of the slain man, whose duty otherwise would have been to slay the slayer. Jesus Himself is our city of refuge, to whom we may flee from the accusation of our sins and their consequences, and the hope we are to lay hold of is that expressed in the Cross, that there is no condemnation to them that are in Christ Jesus. It is in fleeing to Jesus for refuge and laying hold of this hope that we begin the Christian life.

Then, secondly, there is the *"race set before us"* (12:1).

This is the special course marked out for everyone who has begun (not the same course in each case), which he is to run with endurance with no turning back, right to the end.

Thirdly, there is *"the joy set before him"* (12:2). This joy was the Father's reward in glory for His Son for which the Son was prepared to endure all the disgrace of the Cross. Indeed, He is said to have despised the shame of it, that is, to have counted it of little importance in comparison with the joy that awaited Him. The same joy is set before us in our race, because of which joy we too are prepared to endure all sorts of short-term losses because of infinite long-term gains in glory.

This brings us to the last section of the great epistle. It arises directly out of the theme of chapter 10 and its subject extends right through the remaining three chapters.

ENDURANCE

The theme of this final section is "endurance." Its first announcement has been made at the end of chapter 10. Here Paul has been urging the Hebrew Christians not to cast away their confidence which had "great recompence of reward" (10:35). Then he says, "For ye have need of patience, that after ye have done the will of God, ye might receive the promise" (10:36). Now this word *patience* is literally in the Greek "endurance" *(hupomone)*. Indeed, in almost every place where the word *patience* occurs, you can translate it, "endurance." If you make this substitution, you will find it gives a greatly enhanced meaning to the verses in question. "Knowing that tribulation worketh *endurance*" (Rom. 5:3). "If we hope for that we see not, then do we with *endurance* wait for it" (Rom. 8:25). Paul says in 2 Timothy 3:10, "Thou hast fully known my doctrine, manner of life . . . *endurance*, persecutions." James also has much to say of this quality in his epistle: "The trying of your faith worketh *endurance*. But let *endurance* have her perfect work" (1:3,4). Further he says, "Blessed is the man that *endureth* temptation" (1:12), temptation there being not solicitation to evil, but testings and trials. And again: "Behold, we count them happy that *endure*. Ye have heard of the *endurance* of Job . . . " (5:11). Then, the Lord Jesus said to the church at Ephesus: "I know thy works, and thy labour, and thy *endurance*" (Rev. 2:2). And so on.

This important quality, then, is the theme of the last section of the Hebrews epistle. It begins, as we have said, in 10:36 — "Ye have need of *endurance*" — and the word continues to crop up throughout the passage. Moses *"endured*, as seeing him who is invisible" (11:27). "Let us run with *endurance* the race that is set before us" (12:1). Jesus, "for the joy that was set before him, *endured* the cross" (12:2). He *"endured* such contradiction of sinners against himself" (12:3). "If ye *endure* chastening, God dealeth with you as sons" (12:7).

The word has two thoughts contained in it. First, it has the meaning of submission. If one endures persecution or trial, it means he submits to it; he does not run away from it. Then it has the meaning of continuing, of going on undeterred, and of not drawing back. Here we see why it is such an important word, or I should say such an important quality, in the light of the whole message of the epistle. If the only alternative to going on is going back, the opposite of going back is enduring to the end. Indeed, that is exactly the contrast in the first introduction of "endurance" in chapter 10. Having said, "Ye have need of endurance," Paul immediately quotes an Old Testament verse: "But if any man draw back, my soul shall have no pleasure in him" (10:38); and then he adds, "But we are not of them who draw back unto perdition; but of them that believe to the saving of the soul." Obviously, then, the opposite of our drawing back to perdition is our enduring to the end, and thus making "our calling and election sure."

Some time ago I was in another country far from home, ministering the Word, speaking in the same location for six weeks, twice a day, without intermission and without the opportunity to repeat myself, and all that in a situation in which the people were not as responsive as I had hoped. That period seemed an age and I found myself again and again longing to quit. There was, of course, no opportunity to do so, but the desire was in my heart, and that is what God always looks at. As

my wife and I sought the Lord, He spoke the Word to us:
"Behold we count them happy which endure" (James 5:11). As
we went further into the Word, we were surprised to find how
much there was in it on this subject and how essential was this
quality of endurance. And we saw it had the two meanings I
have suggested. We saw it was a call to us to bend the neck to
the situation God had allowed and to the task He had given. By
that I mean we had to surrender what we would wish for
ourselves, and submit to His will as it came to us in His
providences. We saw, too, that it meant going on and on,
undeterred and repenting even when the desire for something
other than what He had given obtruded into our hearts. Not
only did we read, "Ye have need of endurance," but we saw
that it went on to say, " . . . that, after ye have done the will of
God, ye might receive the promise"; and receive the promise
we certainly did. Lives were blessed in those days in a deep
way, as were our own, and we ended praising Him for a new
experience of abounding grace. The test we endured is hardly
worth quoting, as it was so insignificant compared with the
heavy trials that the saints often have to undergo, but I do so
simply to illustrate what this quality of endurance is and how
without it we are all in danger of turning back in one way or
another.

On the other hand, the experience quoted may not be
without application to, say, a pastor in a difficult sphere of
service, a missionary in an unresponsive field, or a layman in an
uncongenial job, any of whom might be tempted to wish to run
away to something else. If that desire is indulged in, it cuts the
nerve of faith for what God has given us to do in the present. He
may have put us in the position in which we are just to learn this
quality of endurance, if for no other reason. Often there are
many other purposes He has in it, blessed ones, but endurance
must be learned first of all.

Only those who have gone on from shadow to substance
will in fact learn this lesson and endure to the end. The promise
of grace on which they have laid hold is to them "an anchor of
the soul, both sure and steadfast, and which entereth into that
within the veil, whither the forerunner is for us entered, even

Jesus, made an high priest for ever after the order of Melchizedek" (6:19,20), from whom they have learned to draw all their life in the midst of a hostile environment; and therefore they endure to the end. Those who have contented themselves with only the shadow Christian life will find their experience fail them when the pressure is applied and they will be in danger of giving up.

THE "WESTMINSTER ABBEY" OF THE BIBLE

It is only after we have been introduced to this theme that we find ourselves moving into the famous chapter 11, which someone has called the "Westminster Abbey" of the Bible, because there lie buried the great Old Testament heroes of faith. But the chapter is not merely a dissertation on the subject of faith, as if dropped in from nowhere. It is introduced here only in pursuit of this main theme of endurance and to show that the only way we can endure to the end against all odds is by faith.

Paul has already linked endurance and faith together in 6:12, where he talks about our becoming "followers of them who through faith and patience inherit the promises." The word *patience* here is not the same as *hupomone* elsewhere, but it means much the same as endurance. Faith apparently is not enough to inherit the promises; it must be faith *and* endurance, as is seen in the case of Abraham, which Paul mentions in verse 15 — who, "after he had patiently endured . . . obtained the promise." On the other hand, if faith must be linked with endurance, the only way to endure is by faith, which is the whole point of introducing Hebrews 11 here.

In this chapter, one particular aspect of faith is stressed. There are, of course, various other aspects of faith in Scripture: faith that is fully persuaded of God's promises (Rom. 4:21), faith that trusts (John 4:50), faith that takes (Luke 18:42), faith that works (James 2:20), and so on. The aspect of faith that is stressed here, however, is none of these. It is rather the faith that endures to the end, and does so in spite of all opposition and suffering, and all because it has "respect to the recompence of the reward."

The chapter begins with a definition of faith from just this point of view. "Faith is the assurance of things hoped for, the conviction of things not seen" (11:1 RSV). Faith has to do with things future and things unseen. The fact that they are not as yet present or seen matters not to faith, provided they are covered by the promises of God. Faith is so assured of the hoped-for blessing and so convinced of the unseen facts that it will venture out on them and, if necessary, will sacrifice present and seen gains in favor of the better things promised. Even if the thing promised does not come to pass in this life, faith is completely assured that there will be a better fulfillment in the next and is still happy to go on enduring to the end, making any sacrifices that will be called for. It does not feel itself cheated that the fulfillment is not until the "better resurrection."

Case after case is quoted of Old Testament men and women of faith, of whom this was true. Sixteen of them are mentioned, together with an unspecified number of prophets. Indeed, Paul says he could tell us of many more, if he had the time ("time would fail me," 11:32).

One thing is said of them all — indeed, it is put both at the beginning and the end of the chapter — "by it the elders had witness borne to them" (11:2) and "these all had witness borne to them through their faith . . ." (11:39). And the witness God gave of them was that they pleased Him. Whatever might have been lacking in their personal characters, the fact that they believed God and acted on His promises was enough to enable Him to express His pleasure with regard to them. God counted their faith a righteousness they did not otherwise possess. That is certainly said of Noah (11:7), and one can assume it goes for the rest of them.

By Faith Suffering Loss

As one looks through the list of characters, one sees that, whereas all demonstrate faith by being assured of things hoped for and convinced of things not seen, some more than others demonstrate the faith that endures to the end and suffers loss to do so. There is Abraham, who by faith left his own country and "went out, not knowing whither he went" (11:8). Then he, Isaac, and Jacob all refrained from building cities that had foundations, preferring to dwell only in tents, which of course had no foundations, because their faith made them look for the better thing God had promised, and they were prepared to await His time. We see Moses, who by faith "refused to be called the son of Pharaoh's daughter" — a big surrender indeed — and "by faith forsook Egypt, not fearing the wrath of the king" (11:24,27). Then there is a nameless company mentioned, people who by faith "were tortured, not accepting deliverance, that they might obtain a better resurrection: and others had trial of cruel mockings and scourgings, yea, moreover of bonds and imprisonment: they were stoned, they were sawn asunder, were tempted, were slain with the sword: they wandered about in sheepskins and goatskins; being destitute, afflicted, tormented; (of whom the world was not worthy:) they wandered in deserts, and in mountains, and in dens and caves of the earth" (11:35-38).

Some by faith obtained promises; others equally by faith did not receive the promise (11:39). Some by faith escaped the edge of the sword (11:34); others equally by faith perished by the sword, because by faith they could not and would not accept release on the terms offered. One way or the other, it was only by faith they were enabled to go through with it to the end and not apostatize. They had faith to believe that Jehovah was standing with them, that there was "a better resurrection" and "a great recompence of reward" hereafter, and they had a determination that at all costs they were not going to miss that.

It can be understood what tremendous bearing this would have on Paul's message to his readers that they should, whatever it might cost them, endure to the end. If it was by faith that the elders did so, this must be the way for them too. This was the great crowd of witnesses, men who had gone this way before, and whose faith was to inspire theirs to see it through.

FINAL SALVATION

Twice it is said in this chapter: "These all died in faith, not having received the promises" (11:13,39). What does this mean? In some cases it meant that the deliverance that was granted to others in this life was not granted to them, and they died expecting a fulfillment in the next life, and were quite content to do so. This word also implies that even those whose faith was rewarded in this life received only a partial fulfillment of the promise. The fullness of what God had in mind for them would not be known until they stood before God beyond the grave — and then not without us of this dispensation (11:40). What a day that will be!

This leads to the truth that the real fulfillment of what God has for us will never be realized in this life, only fully in heaven. Even the most fulfilled Christian life in this world with, say, every hope satisfied and every prayer answered, would be at best but an unfinished symphony. The final movement of the symphony, that which completes the whole, will not sound forth until we stand before the throne of God and of the Lamb in our glorified bodies.

It is always in this sense, in an eschatological sense, that the word *salvation* is used in this epistle (1:14; 9:28). Paul is concerned that his readers should not miss that glorious and final salvation through drawing back to perdition and he points to that "recompence of reward" to nerve them to endure. At all costs, he wants them and us to run with endurance the race set before us.

The Metaphor of the Race

This brings us to another great verse, that at the beginning of chapter 12: "Wherefore seeing we also are compassed about with so great a cloud of witnesses, let us lay aside every weight, and the sin which doth so easily beset us, and let us run with patience the race that is set before us." This verse grows directly out of the previous chapter giving the record of the men and women who endured by faith. This is shown not only by the first word *wherefore*, which obviously points us back to what has just gone before, but also by the clause "seeing we are compassed about by so great a cloud of witnesses." This is not the picture of a stadium filled with spectators who are cheering and encouraging the runners on, as it is sometimes presented.

It is rather a reference to that great company of men and women just mentioned, who were witnesses to the power of faith in their lives and to whom witness was borne by God. What an encouragement such a crowd of witnesses is to us, for we realize that we are not the only ones to have to endure what we are called upon to endure. Moreover, there is also a contemporary cloud of witnesses to encourage us. We do not have to look back only into history to find "the noble army of martyrs"; our own century is probably the age of martyrdom more than any previous one.

Then we come to the metaphor of the race and the call to run it with endurance. This is a metaphor Paul uses on several other occasions in his writings. It refers to the races run at the Grecian games which in the ancient world were held in such high esteem. Another use of this metaphor of the race is found in 1 Corinthians 9:24-27, "Know ye not that they which run in a race run all, but one receiveth the prize?" Then there are his references to himself in 2 Timothy 4:7, "I have finished my course" and Philippians 3:14, "I press toward the mark for the prize of the high calling of God in Christ Jesus"; and also his word to the Galatians: "Ye did run well; who did hinder you" (5:7).

The Christian life, then, is to be regarded as a race and one that is beset with difficulties. For that reason we should perhaps think of it as a cross-country race with fences, ditches, rough fields, and rivers to be traversed, the sort of race that calls for endurance, if ever one does. To have gone on in our spiritual experience from shadow to substance does not exempt us from such a race; rather, it introduces us to it as never before. This is what the reality is all about; it is that, in this arduous race, we have constant access to our living High Priest for the needed staying power. When ours is but the shadow Christian life, our good intentions and our own resources soon vanish away and we want desperately to give up.

In one point the imagery of the race fails us: normally the aim of a race is to compete against others and get ahead of them. Not so the Christian race. Its purpose is just to finish the course; that is feat enough, considering what we often have to bear, not only from the world, but sometimes from false brethren. Paul at the close of his life did not say, "I have finished ahead of all the other Christians," but simply, "I have finished my course." Not everyone who starts on a cross-country race stays the course, but Paul had done so, and that was enough for him to receive the Master's "Well done" — when all too many others had dropped out and finally turned back. It was that possibility of dropping out that leads the apostle to emphasize our theme word: "Let us run with *endurance* the race set before us."

Although in the Christian race we are not competing with one another, Paul tells us in another passage, to which we have already alluded, that we are to run as if only one is going to receive the prize. That means self-discipline and subordinating everything to the one purpose. We are not to amble around the course, being taken up with all sorts of passing interests. Such a person is not going to receive the prize. That brings us to the fact that there is a prize, a crown bestowed at the end of the Christian race, as there was in the Grecian games. The crown bestowed then was not the gold medal of modern Olympic games, but just a wreath put around the victor's head which, of course, soon faded. That is what he alluded to when he said, "They do it to obtain a corruptible crown, but we an incorruptible" (1 Cor. 9:25).

There are, then, rewards and losses in the Christian life, a subject clearly taught in Scripture, but one we do not often hear expounded. Whereas there are those who drop out of the race altogether — those whom we must consider apostates — there are among those who do finish the course differences in the state of grace in which they finish. Notice, I said, state of *grace*, not the state of attainment or of success; this means the degree in which they have appropriated the undeserved grace of God for their poverty. And under grace Jesus warned us that the last may be first and the first last and that there are rewards for the one, and losses for the other.

First Corinthians 3 is the chapter that deals very specially with this matter of rewards and losses for the Christian. The imagery of the Christian life here changes from a race to a building, the foundation of which is Jesus Christ. If a person does not have Him as his foundation, he is not a Christian at all. But the main question here is, What have we built on that foundation, of what sort of material is the superstructure? Ideally, it should be of the same material as the foundation — Christ the foundation and Christ the superstructure. But for all too many of us, whereas the foundation is Christ, the superstructure is largely of the flesh, that is, the actions and reactions and efforts of our self-centered ego. The most hideous thing in the eyes of God must surely be the flesh in His service; and yet our church life is full of it, and nearly all of it unrealized and unjudged.

Well, the time is coming when it is all to be tested by fire. "Every man's work shall be made manifest: for the day shall declare it, because it shall be revealed by fire; and the fire shall try every man's work of what sort it is" (1 Cor. 3:13). There will certainly be rewards in that day: "If any man's work abide which he hath built thereupon, he shall receive a reward" (3:14). But, alas, there will be some losses too, grievous losses: "If any man's work shall be burned, he shall suffer loss: but he himself shall be saved; yet so as by fire" (3:15). I, for one, will be relieved to see some of my service go up in smoke, and only that which was of Christ and of His Holy Spirit remain, for I know there has been all too much that was self-inspired.

LOOKING TO JESUS

Now we come to the supreme motive that inspires us to run with endurance the race that is set before us:

Looking unto Jesus the author and finisher of our faith; who for the joy that was before him endured the cross, despising the shame, and is set down at the right hand of the throne of God. For consider him that endured such contradiction of sinners against himself, lest ye be wearied and faint in your minds. Ye have not yet resisted unto blood, striving against sin (12:2-4).

The believer is to run, looking to Jesus. Usually this is taken to mean that we are to look to Him for help and grace in what we have to undergo. While it is true we have to do so, that is not the meaning here. If we consider the whole of this little passage, it is clear we are to look to Him as the runner's great example of enduring to the very end such things as wrongs, hurts, and insults.

Because some have presented the need to copy the example of Jesus as if it were the way of salvation, those of us who know otherwise have not allowed ourselves to consider Jesus as our example seriously enough. And yet His being our example is presented in Scripture with great power, and always in the context of one thing, what we may call brokenness. His example is cited not as regards ascending to ever greater heights of authority, but rather in His coming down to new depths of humility and of yielding up His rights. This we would all rather not consider, lest we should see that we must go that way too. But there it is, staring us in the face. "Christ also suffered for us, leaving us an example that ye should follow his steps . . . who, when he was reviled, reviled not again; when he suffered, he threatened not; but committed his cause to him that judgeth righteously" (1 Peter 2:21,23), the emphasis here being on nonretaliation, the brokenness that does not stand up for its rights, but lets them go. In John 13:15 Jesus Himself says, "I have given you an example, that ye should do as I have done to you." He is referring here to His taking the place of a servant to wash His disciples' feet, when none of them was willing to do it for the others. He was willing to demean Himself, even if they were not.

Now, here is the same example in Hebrews 12. First, there is the phrase "Jesus, the author and finisher of our faith." The Greek word translated "author" is, literally, the "file-leader" or "pioneer"; and the word translated "finisher" can be read as "fulfillment." In other words, we are to see Jesus as the One who first went this costly way of the endurance of faith for us and the perfect exemplification or fulfillment of it. He is not asking us to go on a path of vilification and misunderstanding (and that may well be our lot sometimes) that He has not already trod in a far deeper degree.

Then, there follows what He endured for us (there is that word *endured* again). "He endured the cross, despising the shame." What Jesus endured, when He could so easily have drawn back from it (twelve legions of angels were awaiting His word), was disgrace, or to use the word given here, shame. Physical suffering is nothing to the pain of disgrace, especially when one is wholly innocent of the grievous imputations of wrong. Jesus endured the disgrace of being regarded as a criminal (for only criminals were put on crosses), when, of course, He was not one at all. And He really endured it, that is, continued with it. He did not protest His innocence; He did not say, what I am sure we would have said, had we been in His place: "I know I am hanging on a cross and it looks as if I am a criminal; but I want to make it quite clear, I am not one. I am not here for any sins of my own, but rather for those of others." He did not say that at all; He just let others think He was a criminal, suffering for His own faults; He just let them "esteem him stricken, smitten of God and afflicted" on His own account (Isa. 53:4). We can hardly bear it when the apostle bids us look away from our little sufferings with their attendant self-pity and hurt feelings to "consider him that endured such contradiction of sinners against himself." Yes, He endured it; He went through with it; He did not say, "I am not going to stand this any longer; I insist that they treat me with the respect due to one in my position." He just bore it, and was not rebellious nor "turned away back" (Isa. 50:5). Then the apostle turns on us with words that cut us to the heart: "Ye have not yet resisted unto blood, striving against sin." Of course we have not! But He has! As He prayed in Gethsemane, "His sweat was as it were great drops of blood, falling down to the ground." O God, forgive us for feeling hurt and resentful over issues which are mere trifles compared with all our File-leader went through for us. O God, have mercy on us for we have "become wearied and faint in our minds" and have wanted to turn back, when the great Captain of our salvation went on and on and on!

The story is told of a British soldier in the first World War, whose nerve broke and who felt he could no longer remain in the front-line trenches. One night he crept away, hoping to make his way to the coast and thence somehow across to England. It was not long before he became lost in the darkness and, seeing what he thought was a signpost, he climbed it and struck a match to see which way it was pointing. As he hung to the crossbar and held his light aloft, he found himself looking into the face of the Crucified; it was a wayside crucifix. That vision of One who had endured so much for him and did not turn back, nerved him to return to those grim trenches and the next day found him with his companions in the place of duty.

But we see in our File-leader the triumph of faith too; for having endured the cross, He "is set down at the right hand of God." We too shall triumph ultimately. The famous protest song of the passive resistance movement in America, "We shall overcome," is more true of the tried and troubled saints than of any other group. In Jesus we are not only on the winning side, but on the side that has already won and we can anticipate this in faith and go forward with buoyancy of spirit.

"Consider Him"; so shalt thou, day by day,
Seek out the lowliest place, and therein stay,
Content to pass away, a thing of nought,
That glory to the Father's Name be brought.

Shrink not, O child of God, but fearless go
Down into death with Jesus: thou shalt know
The power of an endless life begin,
With glorious liberty from self and sin.

"Consider Him," and as you run the race,
Keep ever upward looking at His face,
And thus transformed, illumined thou shalt be,
And Christ's own image shall be seen in thee.

THE CHASTENING OF THE LORD

From this point Paul passes on quite naturally and without a break to speak of the important matter of the chastening of the Lord; it is but an extension of this same theme of endurance. We quote a portion of the passage to give us the gist:

And ye have forgotten the exhortation which speaketh unto you as children, My son, despise not thou the chastening of the Lord, nor faint when thou art rebuked of him: for whom the Lord loveth he chasteneth, and scourgeth every son whom he receiveth. If ye endure chastening, God dealeth with you as with sons; for what son is he whom the father chasteneth not? . . . Shall we not much rather be in subjection to the Father of spirits, and live? . . . Now no chastening for the present seemeth to be joyous, but grievous:

nevertheless afterward it yieldeth the peaceable fruit of righteousness unto them which are exercised thereby. Wherefore lift up the
hands which hang down, and the feeble knees (12:5-7,9,11,12).

As I have said, we are still on the theme of endurance and
Paul tells his readers that they have not only to endure the
hurtful opposition of men as they run the race set before them,
but the loving chastening of the Lord. The latter is just as much
part of the trials of the cross-country race as the former. Indeed, very often they are one and the same. On the one hand,
the difficulties and sufferings come from man; on the other
hand, they could not be happening unless God permitted them
and therefore they come from Him. And coming from Him,
they are to be regarded as part of the chastening and the
discipline which the heavenly Father gives His children.

We are told two things that we are not to do with regard to
His chastening. First, "Despise not thou the chastening of the
Lord," that is, we are not to regard it as of little worth, but
rather to value it highly. We are to look upon it as a mark of His
special affection, "for whom the Lord loveth He chasteneth,"
and we are to seek to learn what He is teaching us through it.
Second, ". . . nor faint when thou art rebuked of Him," that is,
we are not to grow discouraged or give up hope under it, and
certainly not to turn back because of it, for God's intentions in it
are all good. What does discourage us is to think that God must
be punishing us for something when He allows hard things to
happen to us. But God's chastenings are never punitive in their
intention, but only and always restorative. They could not
possibly be considered punishments for sin, because none of
them are severe enough to be so regarded. The only adequate
punishment for sin is what Jesus bore in His body on the tree;
and He has not only borne it, but He has exhausted it.

God's chastenings, then, are designed to restore us to
fuller submission to Himself. Sometimes they are closely associated with sin or rebellion on our part and it is quite clear
wherein God wants us to return. In other situations, it is not
obvious at all. In those cases we must remember that none of us
knows how much was lost in the Fall and that God is on a
recovery operation with all of us, an operation which is not the

work of a day or a year. When we first submitted to Christ, that
was but the beginning of the operation. Even when there is no
active transgression on our part, there are still areas where self
reigns unsuspected and where we must learn to submit more
fully to God. And how can we know that we are submitting to
Him and choosing His will rather than our own, unless that will
sometimes is other than what we would naturally wish for
ourselves. Madame Guyon says that God's will comes to us not
only in His Word, but in His providences, that is, in what He
allows, and that God is always to be found in His will; indeed,
He is to be regarded as virtually identical with it, so that when
we love His will, we are loving Him. In the light of that, most of
us have a long way to go; but God is proceeding apace with His
recovery operation in us and teaching His unwilling pupils how
to choose His will and submit to Him. So Paul says, "Shall we
not much rather be in subjection to the Father of spirits and
live?" (12:9). Yes, there are good lessons to learn in these
experiences — submission to God, if nothing else; but often
much else.

> His purposes will ripen fast,
>   Unfolding every hour:
> The bud may have a bitter taste,
>   But sweet will be the flower.

Little wonder that Paul says that although no chastening
for the present seems to be joyous, but grievous, yet "afterward it yieldeth the peaceable fruit of righteousness unto them
that are exercised thereby" (12:11). But we must be "exercised
thereby." If we are not open to what God has to show us, we
will miss the good thing He designs in it for us.

And so He speaks words of great encouragement to those
of us who are in any degree of trial and chastening. And what
He says is all to one end: "Wherefore lift up the hands which
hang down, and the feeble knees" (12:12), that is, in view of all
the good that comes out of these seasons of trial, there are to be
no attitudes of discouragement, no giving up hope, no turning
back.

And so it is we run with endurance the race that is set
before us, looking to Jesus, our great File-leader, banishing

discouragement, refusing to turn back, counting of small consequence what we have to suffer — and all for the joy that is set before us, the joy of seeing Him face to face, whom, though we have not yet seen Him as we shall see Him then, we have loved all the way through.

> It will be worth it all
>   When we see Jesus.
> Life's trials will seem so small
>   When we see Him.
> One glimpse of His dear face
> All sorrows will erase.
> So let us run the race
> Till we see Christ.

THE FINAL DOXOLOGY

The closing one and a half chapters are filled with further encouragements, warnings, injunctions, and admonitions, all of them glorious, till our beloved brother Paul (and he has become beloved to us, hasn't he?) concludes with one of the greatest doxologies in the Bible:

> Now the God of peace, that brought again from the dead our Lord Jesus, that great shepherd of the sheep, through the blood of the everlasting covenant, make you perfect in every good work to do his will, working in you that which is well-pleasing in his sight, through Jesus Christ; to whom be glory for ever and ever. Amen (13:20,21).

Appendix:
The Versions Used

Appendix:

The Versions Used

A WORD NEEDS to be added about the particular versions of the Scriptures which have been used in this book. The basic text that has been used throughout is the King James Version, or as it is also called in Britain, the Authorised Version. It is still the most widely used one in the English-speaking world today. Its courtly Elizabethan English makes it to my mind by far the most attractive. It may come as a surprise to some to know that it is one of the most literal of the translations and gives more of a word-for-word rendering than almost any other; you can nearly always be sure that for every word in the English text there is a corresponding Hebrew or Greek word in the original. Where an English word is used in the King James Version for which there is not an actual one in the original (sometimes it is necessary to insert an English word to give a sentence completion), the word is put in italics, so we may know the word has been added. All this is very helpful to the careful student of the Scriptures, who above all wants to know accurately what the writers originally wrote. He is then free to make his own paraphrases and amplifications if he needs to, as he absorbs its message into his own heart, or expounds it to the people to whom he is sent.

Even in some of its obscurities, the King James Version is to be commended; if in a few places its translation is obscure, it is invariably because the sentence in the original is obscure through, say, some mutilation of the text in transmission. It seldom makes a judicious guess as to what it was meant to be, which leaves the reader free to come to his own conclusions, as he compares other versions. There are admittedly in the King James Version certain archaic words and expressions no longer in current use today. But the diligent student, who is out first of all for accuracy, will easily tolerate these, and in any case, it is not difficult for him to ascertain their modern equivalent.

When I extol the accuracy of the King James Version, I include with it its twin sons, the Revised Version of 1885 and the American Standard Version of 1901. In the 1880s it was decided that the King James Version should be revised in the interests of even greater accuracy. But the brief given to the two translating committees, one English and the other American, was that they should change the language and tone of the King James Version as little as possible, consistent with their commission to achieve a greater accuracy where needed. The two committees did a splendid job. The translation remained in essence the King James Version, but with certain very considerable gains. There were, however, a number of places where the English and American committees failed to agree in their translation. So it was decided to publish their versions separately, the English one in 1885 and the American one a few years later, with each version containing a list of the places in which it differed from the other. Examination of these differences shows them to be slight, so that it was virtually the same revision of the King James Version on both sides of the Atlantic — with one great exception. The American Standard Version put the name "Jehovah" in those places where this sacred, personal name of God appeared in the Hebrew, instead of translating it as LORD, as all other versions before and since have done.

The reason for this reticence to use the name of Jehovah stems from the ancient Jewish tradition that this, the personal name of God, was too sacred to use and they always read

Adonai, "Lord," instead. All the other versions up to the present time have followed suit, but most of them have written the word LORD all in capitals when it is "Jehovah" (or *Yahweh)* in the original. The American revisers in the 1880s decided otherwise, and wherever "Jehovah" appears in the original, it is put as such in the English. The King James Version had used that beautiful name but seven times; in the American Standard Version it is everywhere, and by seeing it in its many contexts we understand it to be preeminently the name of grace. This makes this version, in my view, tower above all other versions as the noblest of them all. The use of the name of Jehovah wherever it appears in the original gives immense, additional power and meaning to many an already-glorious Old Testament passage.

Whereas the version used in this writing is basically the King James Version, I have substituted here and there preferred readings from these other versions — its two children, the Revised Version and the American Standard Version — and have done so without burdening the reader with information as to which word, phrase, or sentence comes from which version. Sometimes the word or phrase chosen is from the margin of these versions. The reader then can take it that the end result is an amalgamation of these three related versions, which I believe gives as clear and accurate a reading as can be obtained.

In addition, there are quotations in the body of the chapters here and there from the Revised Standard Version, where I have thought it throws further light on a passage. In every place where that version is quoted, I have been careful to state the fact; such quotations are used by permission of the copyright holder, the National Council of the Churches of Christ in the U.S.A. Even in using the Revised Standard Version, I have not departed from the family of the King James Version, for the Revised Standard Version is itself a revision of the American Standard Version, which in turn is a revision of the King James Version. So there we have the family tree — the King James Version, the father; the Revised Version and the American Standard Version, the twin sons; and the Revised

Standard Version, the grandson. In spite of the use of all four versions, the fact remains that this book is basically an exposition of the epistle in the King James Version, and these other versions are used only occasionally to elucidate it.

My comments on the matter of the more literal translations do not for a moment suggest that the various modern versions, some of which have much more the character of a paraphrase, are not of real value and usefulness. None can deny that God is using them greatly to the blessing of new classes of readers. But the Christian who has a hunger to study in depth these wonderful Scriptures God has given us and to lay hold of the fullness of their message will need sooner or later to graduate from the paraphrase versions to the more literal ones in order to get as close as he can to the original and thus be able to dig out for himself the gold that is there. Such in-depth study of the Scriptures is not merely for preachers. Every Christian who is growing in grace at all should be possessed with a spiritual hunger that will make him a lifelong student of the Scriptures and that in ever greater depth.